One Another
The Community God Wants Us to Be

Eddie Rasnake

Copyright © 2019 Eddie Rasnake

All rights reserved. No part of this book may be reproduced in any form without the expressed written consent of the copyright owner.

DEDICATION

This book is dedicated to the local fellowship of believers known as Woodland Park Baptist Church, with whom I am privileged to share community as we do life together.

Books by Eddie Rasnake:

What Should I Do, Lord?
One Another: The Community God Wants Us To Be

Working Thru The Word Series:
Colossians
Jude
James
Psalms
2 Corinthians
Righteousness of the Heart (The Sermon on the Mount – Matthew 5-7)
Radical Christianity (The Upper Room Discourse – John 13-17)
Dangers to Devotion (Letters to the 7 Churches – Revelation 2-3)

Discipleship Series:
Becoming a Disciple
Becoming a Discipler
Becoming an Elder
God's Will
Transforming Truths
The Miraculous Gifts

Following God Bible Study Series:
First Steps for the New Christian
Living God's Will
Ephesians
Romans
The Acts of the Holy Spirit 1 (1-12)
The Acts of the Holy Spirit 2 (13-28)
Using Your Spiritual Gifts
How to Develop a Quiet Time
Spiritual Warfare

Following God: Co-Authored with Wayne Barber and Rick Shepherd
Women of the Bible – Book 1
Women of the Bible – Book 2
Life Principles from the Old Testament
Kings of the Old Testament
Prophets of the Old Testament
Men of the New Testament
Life Principles for Worship from the Tabernacle

Co-Authored with Michele Rasnake
Held in His Grace: A Young Mother's Journey Through Cancer

CONTENTS

	Introduction	i
1	Week 1: Pray For One Another	9
2	Week 2: Put One Another First	25
3	Week 3: Bear One Another's Burdens	40
4	Week 4: Encourage One Another	56
5	Week 5: Be Accountable to One Another	71
6	Week 6: Forgive One Another	87
7	Week 7: Minister To One Another	102
8	Week 8: Love One Another	118

Introduction

Imagine you have just met that perfect someone. That person is everything you have been looking for in a relationship. As you get to know them, your love for him or her grows, and you imagine spending the rest of your life with them. How would you develop a FANTASTIC relationship with that special someone? Would you say, "Boy, it sure was good meeting you – I hope we see each other once in a while"? You would probably not be passive and would not leave your time together to chance. Instead, you would seek them out and get to know that person better. You would make your time together a priority. You would place extreme importance on your communication with that person – in short, you would pursue them. This is the plan of action we should use to get to know God. Take a moment to look back over this paragraph and think about your relationship with God. This example answers the "how" of pursuing God. But there is a more fundamental question which must be answered first – Why?

If you had a chance to meet with the President of the United States, you would make sure you did not miss such a great opportunity. You would rearrange your schedule, say "no" to other commitments, make any sacrifice necessary, and take advantage of the opportunity. The President is too significant to reject, but Jehovah is far greater than any political power or presidential office. We have been invited into the presence of the King of kings. The greatness of God should motivate us because He is more worthy of my time and attention than anything else. Time with Him satisfies the deepest needs and longings of our hearts, and at the same time, causes us to long for more.

Becoming a Christian isn't all there is to a relationship with God, just as a wedding ceremony isn't all there is to being married; it is merely the beginning. We must spend time with God in order to grow closer to Him. We must follow Him. Perhaps it is the fact that the opportunity to pursue God is always present that keeps us from taking advantage of it as we should.

Each believer is a disciple of Jesus Christ, and the word disciple means follower. Each Christian is either a good disciple (follower) or a bad one. The goal of every disciple should be continual growth as a faithful follower and developing a more intimate relationship with God as a branch does with the vine. John 15:7-8 tells us that the foundation of being a disciple is abiding in Him and having His words abide in us.

The saints of old often called this pursuit a "quiet time" or personal devotions – spending time with God, listening to what He has to say, and talking with Him honestly from our hearts. Time with God should involve Bible study – and certainly we should study the Scriptures – but Bible study cannot be simply an intellectual pursuit of information; it should be the foundation of relationship. As we read and study the Word of God, we must at the same time pursue the God of the Word, and He will guide us into true community.

*NOTE: Take time to highlight or underline any parts of each day's reading that spoke to you personally

WEEK ONE
"Pray for One Another"

Day 1: The Prayer Connection

"Therefore, confess your sins to one another, and <u>pray for one another</u>, so that you may be healed. The effective prayer of a righteous man can accomplish much."

- James 5:16

James 5:16 commands us to "pray for one another." It is an imperative statement. It is not a suggestion. Also, the Greek verb there is in the present tense. That means we are to continually pray for each other, not just pray once and forget it. God wants His church to be connected to each other and dependent on Him. The word translated "pray" used here is *euchomai* and has the idea of a **strong desire** for someone – to express a wish. Consider the relational implications of this. We should be involved in each other's lives so that we know how to pray for each other. We should care enough to be able to recognize the needs of those in our lives and to have developed a "wish" for their good. If so, we will be motivated to express that wish to One who can do something about it. Communicating that awareness to God is to be a habitual manifestation of our dependence on Him. We recognize what we are unable to do, and we exercise faith in what He is able to do. You see, praying for each other is a three-way exchange: God, the other person, and me. The other person has a need. If it is worthy of prayer, it is beyond that person's ability to address. I also have a need. God desires that we live in moment-by-moment dependence on Him. Therefore, I must to pray so that I entrust the need to God instead of to the other person or to myself. If the church is to be a body, I also need to hurt. I need to mourn with those who are mourning. When the church is a "One Another" community, we all share in the pleasures of each **and** the pains of each as well. God even instructs "confess your sins to one another." We need to be open enough with each other – even to the point of sharing our faults – so that our truest and deepest needs are known. We must be willing to be vulnerable with one another.

I have learned that prayer is one of the ways God knits the body together. When I am praying for another, I develop compassion for their predicament. To pray rightly, I must place myself in their shoes. While this influences how I pray, it also affects how I view and relate with them. God knows that. He desires that our lives be connected to Him **and** to each other. In the above passage, James promises that "the effective prayer of a righteous man can accomplish much." The Greek word for prayer here (*deesis*) is an entirely different word than the one first mention. This word carries the idea of **acknowledging a need** and asking God to meet that need. What a beautiful consideration when we think of one another. We should have a strong desire for God to work in the lives of those around us. We should want to see His will accomplished, and His joy and peace made real in their lives. As we see needs that the person cannot meet – needs that only God can truly meet in the right way and at the right time – we call to the Lord on their behalf. If we can learn to pray with this kind of care for one another, we will often see heaven on earth. That is what God wants. He wants His will in each life. He wants each of us admitting that we cannot meet the needs we see. He wants us coming to Him to meet the need His way since He knows best in *every situation* for *each person*. How aware are you of the needs around you in the body? How open are you with your own needs?

Food for thought

God wants His church to be a community that is connected to each other and dependent upon Him.

ACTS PRAYING

When we talk with God, what should we speak about? I have always found the "ACTS" acrostic as a good guide for prayer. In this system, the letters "A-C-T-S" stand for adoration, confession, thanksgiving and supplication. All are types of prayer admonished in Scripture, but I think this order is important. By beginning with adoration – we start with our eyes on God instead of ourselves. Confession should naturally flow out of focusing on who God is. With our eyes on Him, we will be sensitive to anything that stands between us and Him. Thanksgiving should come before supplication. We should be mindful of what God has already done before requesting what we would like to see Him do. I offer this as a general guideline for talking with God.

A - **ADORATION** - Take some time to praise God for who He is, identifying some of His attributes you find particularly meaningful. You may want to express your heart to Him in a journal. Personally, I have found writing these thoughts out in my journal is so helpful to my worship, for my conscience will not allow me to write words I know that I do not really mean.

C - **CONFESSION** - Remember, don't go looking for something to confess; that is introspection. Instead ask God to search your heart and to bring to mind anything that needs to be dealt with.

T - **THANKSGIVING** - Thank God for the many blessings of your life and take a moment to ask God what you need to be thankful for.

S - **SUPPLICATION** - Pray for God to working in your life as you seek to assume your role in helping the body become the kind of community God desires. Bring to Him any requests and needs that are on your heart.

Day 2: The Four "Alls" of Prayer

"With all prayer and petition pray at all times in the Spirit, and with this in view, be on the alert with all perseverance and petition for all the saints."

- Ephesians 6:18

Through the gift of supplication, we can enter into the needs of others. We can travel great distances on our knees. The word "all" is used four times in Ephesians 6:18, and each use instructs us about prayer. The first "all" of prayer is that "all prayer and petition" must be "in the Spirit." Prayer is talking with God. This may sound overly simplistic, but it is easily forgotten. Prayer is a conversation between our spirit and the Spirit of God. But if I am not careful, it can become a habit or ritual of speaking words that do not make it past the ceiling. What constitutes true prayer is not determined by folded hands, closed eyes, or bowed heads. True prayer happens when I am honestly praying from my heart and I am really talking to God. Sometimes what we call prayer is merely talking to ourselves in religious jargon or talking to the others around us in spiritual sounding sermonettes. Real prayer is talking with God and God alone.

The second "all" of prayer is that I am to "pray at all times." Prayer is not reserved for a special hour of the day or a special meeting on the church calendar. God intends our praying to be an ongoing, unending conversation between us and the One who will never leave us (Hebrews 13:5). The apostle Paul exhorted the Thessalonian believers, "pray without ceasing" (1 Thessalonians 5:17). That is not possible if prayer is something which occurs at a particular hour or a meeting. But it is possible if it is something which happens in our hearts. We can converse with Christ as we walk, as we wait, as we work, and even as we worry – especially then. From the time we awaken, we should be talking with the Lord. This kind of praying isn't meant for flowery words or long monologues. It may be as simple as saying "Lord, I need your help." When are we to pray? At all times.

The third "all" of prayer is "with all perseverance." Prayer is not preparation for the work of ministry, it is the work of ministry and believe me, it is work. The great preacher and intercessor R. A. Torrey wrote, "Why is it that God does not give to us the things that we ask, the first time we ask? The answer is plain: He would do us the far greater good of training us in persistent faith...Oh, men and women, pray through; pray through; pray through! Do not just begin to pray and pray a little while and throw up your hands and quit; but pray and pray and pray until God bends the heavens and comes down!"

The fourth "all" of prayer is "petition for all the saints." Prayer is not to be selfish or self-serving. God wants His body to be a community that cares for one another through prayers for one another. If the only needs I discuss are my own, I am not praying the way God wants. He wants us to be lifting up each other. This even includes the ones I don't like – especially those. If my attitude toward a fellow brother or sister is stained or strained, praying for them helps both of us immensely. In 1 Corinthians 12:25 Paul puts forward the goal that "there may be no division in the body, but that the members may have the same care for one another." We need to pray for those we don't want to pray for. In the Sermon on the Mount Jesus said, "But I say to you, love your enemies and pray for those who persecute you" (Matthew 5:44). Through prayer, we can work to turn enemies into friends.

Food for thought

God wants His body to be a community that cares for one another through prayers for one another.

ACTS PRAYING

A - **ADORATION** - Take some time to praise God for who He is, identifying some of His attributes you find particularly meaningful.

C - **CONFESSION** - Remember, don't go looking for something to confess; that is introspection. Instead ask God to search your heart and to bring to mind anything that needs to be dealt with.

T - **THANKSGIVING** - Thank God for the many blessings of your life, taking a moment to ask God what you need to be thankful for.

S - **SUPPLICATION** - Pray for God's working in your life as you seek to assume your role in helping the body become the community God desires. Bring to Him any requests and needs that are on your heart.

Day 3: The Sin of Unspoken Supplication

"Moreover, as for me, far be it from me that I should sin against the Lord by ceasing to pray for you; but I will instruct you in the good and right way. Only fear the Lord and serve Him in truth with all your heart; for consider what great things He has done for you."

- 1 Samuel 12:23

Have you ever told someone, "I'll be praying for you" and didn't? My guess is that we all have done this many times. Our intentions are good, but memory and other distractions may inhibit intentions from becoming reality. We may feel a moment of guilt when we see the person, or we may forget about the incident altogether. We probably wouldn't think of our neglect as "sin." That is what makes Samuel's words here so intriguing. He speaks of his potential failure to pray for the people of Israel as a sin, and not just a sin against Israel. He calls it a sin against God. The context of Samuel's words here are the transition from the period of the judges to the time of the kings and prophets. Samuel was really the bridge between those two eras, serving as the last judge and the first prophet as the first king was installed. Look at the words Samuel uses to convey his heart. Samuel considered it sin to ever stop praying for Israel. We often think of sin as something wrong that we do, but here Samuel defines it as sin being something left undone. Are we guilty of the sin of unspoken supplication?

There are many VIP's in our life that God would have us to pray for. Obviously, we should pray for our family and cherished friends. No one will pray as passionately for them as we would. We see from Samuel's example that we must pray regularly for those under our spiritual charge. Perhaps the Lord has given us a Bible study group or Sunday School class, or we may be in charge of a church. Even if we aren't, we should pray for the one to which we belong. We see Paul and other spiritual leaders repeatedly say, "Pray for us" (e.g. 1 Thessalonians 5:25, 2 Thessalonians 3:1, Hebrews 13:18, etc.). We have a responsibility to pray for those who lead us spiritually, as well as those whom we lead. We also have a vested interest, for if they are doing well, we benefit, and if they are not, we suffer. We lose the benefit we would have if God were ministering to us through them, or we add the burden of more needed ministry and concern if they are under our charge. This kind of praying is what I call "prayer along the vertical line." We are to pray for those over us and for those under us.

The vertical line of prayer is important, but it is not the only one that should shape our praying. As we are seeing in the "One Another" commands, there is a horizontal line we should also be concerned with. We should pray for one another – our fellow Christians. Writing to the Thessalonians, Paul talked of his prayers of thanks for them: "We ought always to give thanks to God for you, brethren…because your faith is greatly enlarged, and the love of each one of you toward one another grows ever greater." Praying for one another helps cement our love for each other. God wants His church to be a community where we don't just say we will pray for each other; we really do pray. This is especially true if they ask us to pray. I always try to either pray with them right then if appropriate, or to start praying as soon as the conversation has ended. Our supplication matters. We may not always see the difference, but it always makes a difference. Revelation 5:8 speaks of "golden bowls full of incense, which are the prayers of the saints." These are kept in the presence of the Lord in heaven. That idea ought to motivate us away from the sin of unspoken supplication.

Food for thought

God wants His church to be a community where we don't just say we will pray for each other; we really do pray.

ACTS PRAYING

A - **ADORATION** - Take some time to praise God for who He is, identifying some of His attributes you find particularly meaningful.

C - **CONFESSION** - Remember, don't go looking for something to confess; that is introspection. Instead ask God to search your heart and to bring to mind anything that needs to be dealt with.

T - **THANKSGIVING** - Thank God for the many blessings of your life, taking a moment to ask God what you need to be thankful for.

S - **SUPPLICATION** - Pray for God's working in your life as you seek to assume your role in helping the body become the community God desires. Bring to Him any requests and needs that are on your heart.

Day 4: Bestowing Favor Through Prayer

"For we do not want you to be unaware, brethren, of our affliction which came to us in Asia, that we were burdened excessively, beyond our strength, so that we despaired even of life; indeed, we had the sentence of death within ourselves so that we would not trust in ourselves, but in God who raises the dead; who delivered us from so great a peril of death, and will deliver us, He on whom we have set our hope. And He will yet deliver us, you also joining in helping us through your prayers, so that thanks may be given by many persons on our behalf for the favor bestowed on us through the prayers of many."

- 2 Corinthians 1:8-11

In this passage we see that God does allow even His greatest servants to be hard pressed with difficulty. Listen to how Paul describes their experience in Asia. He and his traveling companions were "burdened excessively." They were taken beyond their strength. It got so bad at some point during their difficulties that Paul says they "despaired even of life." Death looked better than what they were going through. But Paul also had come to a place of recognizing that the adversity brought a good result as well. It made them unable to trust in themselves to deliver. The situation was beyond their control. That may not sound good, but it made them put their trust in God instead of themselves. As Geoffrey Bull says, "self-reliance, is God-defiance." He doesn't want us to be able to handle life by ourselves.

When Paul speaks of God as "He on whom we have set our hope," he is still waiting for deliverance. "And He will yet deliver us," was his expectation. How could he be so confident? Because he had people praying for him. Paul didn't want the Corinthians "to be unaware, brethren, of our affliction," because he needed them to pray for him. I wonder how many times our deliverance has been delayed because we were not willing to share the need with the body. We didn't let our need be known or request the needed prayers. God can do whatever He wants whenever He wants, but sometimes He chooses to wait for us to exercise the faith of casting our cares on Him before He intervenes. God wants His church to be a community where we bear each other's burdens in prayer because "we, who are many, are one body in Christ, and individually members one of another" (Romans 12:5).

Did you notice what Paul reveals here about the impact of the Corinthian prayers? Their intercession was more than just moral support. He says to them, "you also joining in helping us through your prayers." When you pray for one another, do you believe that your prayers make a difference? You should, because they do. One of the reasons God wants to work through our joining with others in supplication is so that we all get to rejoice in the answers. Paul's expectation is "that thanks may be given by many persons on our behalf for the favor bestowed upon us through the prayers of many." Did you catch that last phrase? He said there was "favor bestowed upon us through the prayers of the many." But what if the many weren't praying? God wants us to "own" the hardships of others in the body. He wants us to pray for one another so He can bestow favor through our prayers. Paul did think it was important to acknowledge that God was the one who would "yet deliver," but the Corinthians had the privilege of joining God in what He wanted to do in the lives of others. We have that privilege as well. God wants us joining Him through prayer. Is there someone you can bestow favor on through prayer? God may be waiting for you to join Him before their deliverance is sent.

Food for thought

God wants His church to be a community where we bear each other's burdens in prayer for one another

ACTS PRAYING

A - **ADORATION** - Take some time to praise God for who He is, identifying some of His attributes you find particularly meaningful.

C - **CONFESSION** - Remember, don't go looking for something to confess; that is introspection. Instead ask God to search your heart and to bring to mind anything that needs to be dealt with.

T - **THANKSGIVING** - Thank God for the many blessings of your life, taking a moment to ask God what you need to be thankful for.

S - **SUPPLICATION** - Pray for God's working in your life as you seek to assume your role in helping the body become the community God desires. Bring to Him any requests and needs that are on your heart.

Day 5: Waiting in Prayer

"When they [the disciples] had entered the city, they went up to the upper room where they were staying…These all with one mind were continually devoting themselves to prayer"

- Acts 1:13-14

Jesus' words to the disciples before His ascension had not been vague or ambiguous. Wait! Ten days separated His ascension and the coming of the Holy Spirit. The disciples spent those days praying. When we pray, rest assured there will be times when we have to wait for the answer. It is frustrating how often that word "wait" appears in Scripture, but there is much spirituality woven into this simple term. When you think about it, much of life is spent waiting. But waiting is not something we do until life happens – it is part of life. We can accept that most of our prayers are not answered instantly. We struggle is when God takes longer to act than we think He should. I believe God has purpose in the waiting part of prayer. There is something in waiting that draws our eyes to Him where they should be. The longer we pray, the more God reshapes what we are praying for and molds it toward His will. Waiting on the Lord focuses us in making sure we are seeking God and staying sensitive to Him. Likely part of that time in the Upper Room was praying <u>for</u> one another – that is our theme this week – but an important point not to miss is that they were praying <u>with</u> one another.

One danger when we are waiting on a response to our prayers is to lose heart and stop praying. When God doesn't answer right away, we think we have wasted our time. Horatius Bonar reminds us, "No prayer is lost. Praying breath was never spent in vain. There is no such thing as prayer unanswered or unnoticed by God, and some things that we count as refusals or denials are simply delays." In this passage we find that the disciples were "continually devoting themselves" to prayer – a strong expression denoting persistence.

Perhaps God's delay was so they would persist. Sooner or later, each one of us finds ourselves in the place of waiting. One practical lesson we glean from Acts chapter one is that it is easier to be devoted to prayer with others than alone. These disciples prayed together. Not only is praying together a help and encouragement to you – it is also a ministry to the other person. As Jesus prayed in Gethsemane, He asked the disciples to stay and pray with Him. Unfortunately, they weren't very persistent. In Mark 14:37-38 we read, "And He came and found them sleeping, and said to Peter, 'Simon, are you asleep? Could you not keep watch for one hour?' Keep watching and praying that you may not come into temptation; the spirit is willing, but the flesh is weak." We need each other if we are to "keep watching and praying." Maybe there is a prayer meeting or prayer chain at your church that you could get connected with. Or perhaps you could ask another believer to join with you as a prayer partner. The ten days between the ascension of Jesus and Pentecost represented "wait training" for the disciples. An important part of this "wait training" was focused prayer. It is this unseen activity that makes such a difference in each of our situations. E. M. Bounds wrote, "It is true that Bible prayers in word and print are short, but the praying men of the Bible were with God through many a sweet and holy wrestling hour. They won by few words but long waiting." Such praying makes a difference in us as a body. Luke records that they prayed "with one mind." Paul twice exhorted the Romans to "be of the same mind toward one another" (Romans 12:16; 15:5). One of the benefits of praying with one another is that God knits our hearts together in unity.

Food for thought

God wants His body to be a community that waits before Him in unified prayer.

ACTS PRAYING

A - **ADORATION** - Take some time to praise God for who He is, identifying some of His attributes you find particularly meaningful.

C - **CONFESSION** - Remember, don't go looking for something to confess; that is introspection. Instead ask God to search your heart and to bring to mind anything that needs to be dealt with.

T - **THANKSGIVING** - Thank God for the many blessings of your life, taking a moment to ask God what you need to be thankful for.

S - **SUPPLICATION** - Pray for God's working in your life as you seek to assume your role in helping the body become the community God desires. Bring to Him any requests and needs that are on your heart.

WEEK TWO
"Put One Another First"

Day 1: Regarding One Another as More Important

"Do nothing from selfishness or empty conceit, but with humility of mind let each of you regard one another as more important than himself; do not merely look out for your own personal interests, but also for the interests of others. Have this attitude in yourselves which was also in Christ Jesus"

- Philippians 2:3-5

What is your attitude toward others in the church? Does it reflect the humble mindset which sees others as more important or does your attitude communicate that you are the most important person in each relationship? Notice, I am not asking about your actions – how you treat others. I am talking about your attitude – what you think in your heart about others. As Christians, we probably are conditioned to SAY that others are more important, but that only lasts until our rights are impinged upon. Then our attitude reveals itself. Chuck Swindoll has this to say about "attitude"—"The longer I live the more convinced I become that life is 10 percent what happens to us and 90 percent how we respond to it." That's a pretty clear statement about the importance of our attitude. When Paul wrote Philippians 2, he had plenty of opportunity to have a bad attitude. He was imprisoned in Rome because of the lies of his enemies, yet his attitude was sterling – he had no complaints. The Lord was with him and he ministered to soldiers and to many, many visitors who came to see him and to listen to him teach and preach about Jesus and the

Kingdom of God (Acts 28:30-31). He was living out what he wrote to the Romans: "Be devoted to one another in brotherly love; give preference to one another in honor" (Romans 12:10).

In those dark circumstances, Paul experienced the encouragement of Christ and the love and fellowship of the Spirit (2:1). There he discovered the joy of humility – of what it means to regard others as more important – and of serving others' interests and not just his own (2:3). When he thought about the matter of mindset or attitude, he thought of Christ whose heart and mindset were perfect. Christ was willing to take the form of a bondservant to serve others even to the point of death on a Roman cross. He gave His life serving His Father and us.

When Christ is our Life (as He was for Paul—Philippians 1:21), and when we are walking surrendered to Him, we will experience that same encouragement and love of Christ as well as the fellowship of the Spirit that Paul mentions in Philippians 2:1. These are the basis of a right relationship with others which he begins talking about in verse 2—a relationship marked by oneness of mind and heart, by *agape* love, by a unity of spirit and a oneness of purpose (everyone has the same goal). That is also the basis of **a right attitude toward one another**—verses 3 and 4. When Christ is our Life, people are not a problem. They are our opportunity to express humility, genuine love, and a servant's heart in looking out for their needs. Paul goes on to talk about two men who showed this same kind of attitude. Not only do we see it in Christ, we see it in Timothy and Epaphroditus (2:19-30).

Food for thought

Do you have the attitude in yourself that was also in Christ Jesus?

ACTS PRAYING

A - **ADORATION** - Take some time to praise God for who He is, identifying some of His attributes you find particularly meaningful. You may want to express your heart to Him in a journal.

C - **CONFESSION** - Remember, don't go looking for something to confess; that is introspection. Instead ask God to search your heart and to bring to mind anything that needs to be dealt with.

T - **THANKSGIVING** - Thank God for the many blessings of your life, taking a moment to ask God what you need to be thankful for.

S - **SUPPLICATION** - Pray for God to working in your life as you seek to assume your role in helping the body become the kind of community God desires. Bring to Him any requests and needs that are on your heart.

Day 2: Laying Down Self

"Greater love has no one than this, that one lay down his life for his friends."

- John 15:13

In John 15:12, Jesus told His disciples, "This is My commandment, that you love one another, just as I have loved you." He followed this up by clarifying that the greatest act of love one could do was to lay down his life for others. On December 4, 2006, Manning a .50-caliber machine gun in the turret of a Humvee in Iraq, Pfc. Ross McGinnis could see the insurgent fling a hand grenade at his vehicle from a rooftop. He shouted and tried to deflect it, but it fell inside near four of his buddies. What followed was a stunning act of self-sacrifice. McGinnis, a 19-year-old from rural Pennsylvania and the youngest soldier in his unit, threw himself backward onto the grenade, absorbing the blast with his body. He was killed instantly. The others escaped serious injury.[1] Private McGinnis was posthumously awarded the Medal of Honor, and rightly so. We hold such sacrifice in awe. He literally laid down his life for his friends. Ross McGinnis' example extends far beyond his one final act of self-sacrifice. In a statement released by his parents, we are told: "Ross did not become OUR hero by dying to save his fellow soldiers from a grenade. He was a hero to us long before he died, because he was willing to risk his life to protect the ideals of freedom and justice that America represents... The lives of four men who were his Army brothers outweighed the value of his one life. It was just a matter of simple kindergarten arithmetic. Four means more than one. It didn't matter to Ross that he could have escaped the situation without a scratch. Nobody would have questioned such a reflex reaction. What mattered to him were the four men placed in his care on a moment's notice. One moment he was responsible for defending the rear of the convoy from enemy fire; the next moment he held the lives of four

---

[1] http://www.washingtonpost.com/wp-dyn/content/article/2007/01/01/AR2007010100759.html

of his friends in his hands."[2] He was already living a life of putting the welfare and safety of others ahead of his own. It was his lifestyle of laying down himself for others that made the decision of an instant his natural reflex. Were he accustomed to living selfishly, he would have reacted differently.

As difficult as it would be for any of us to make that huge choice of a moment to sacrifice our lives to save others, in some ways it is even more difficult to make the little choices every day to put others first. Those are not dramatic, life-or-death decisions. Yet they shape the measure of our character. Jesus commanded us to love one another. In this same conversation, He said, "You did not choose Me but I chose you, and appointed you that you would go and bear fruit, and that your fruit would remain, so that whatever you ask of the Father in My name He may give to you" (John 15:16). What kind of fruit does Christ want us to bear? "This I command you, that you love one another" (John 15:17).

---

[2] http://www.washingtonpost.com/wp-dyn/content/article/2007/01/01/AR2007010100760.html

ONE ANOTHER

Food for thought

Who comes first, you, or others?

ACTS PRAYING

A - **ADORATION** - Take some time to praise God for who He is, identifying some of His attributes you find particularly meaningful. You may want to express your heart to Him in a journal.

C - **CONFESSION** - Remember, don't go looking for something to confess; that is introspection. Instead ask God to search your heart and to bring to mind anything that needs to be dealt with.

T - **THANKSGIVING** - Thank God for the many blessings of your life, taking a moment to ask God what you need to be thankful for.

S - **SUPPLICATION** - Pray for God to working in your life as you seek to assume your role in helping the body become the kind of community God desires. Bring to Him any requests and needs that are on your heart.

Day 3: Using Our Gifts

"But to each one is given the manifestation of the Spirit for the common good."

- 1 Corinthians 12:7

What do you expect of a "gifted" person? In our culture, a "gifted" athlete or musician is applauded and admired. A "gifted" leader usually is rewarded handsomely by his employer. When we encounter the "gifted", we expect them to be given prominence, and often they expect that as well. You can understand how the non-Christian would think that. If one does not believe in God, and believes that we are all products of a Darwinian evolutionary process, then all accomplishments are attained by personal merit. We may use the term "gifted", but we really mean "earned." This "survival of the fittest" mentality champions the victor and forgets the vanquished. When we understand that we are not self-made, but have been created by God, everything appears in a different light. Our areas of giftedness must be recognized as just that – gifts. Years ago someone shared with me that they had been blessed by my teaching. They asked, "What is the secret to how much more you get when you study than I do. Are you just a really diligent student?" As I reflected on the question, in honesty I had to humbly confess, "No, I'm really not what you would call diligent." My teaching was my greatest contribution to them, and if God had "gifted" me, I couldn't even take credit for it. I had to recognize that whatever I had to offer another was because of Him, not me.

We must recognize the purpose for which our gifts were given. God wants His body to use our gifts and talents for the common good instead of living selfishly. We were never intended to be the sole beneficiaries of our giftedness. God blessed us with whatever talents we have – whether our abilities are athletic, musical, public speaking, intelligence, or business savvy – and He did so in order to make us a blessing to others. God desires that every believer be a minister, and not just a ministry. Not all of us will preach sermons or serve in vocational ministry, but each of us can be used of God to minister to someone else. If we have truly been born again, we have each been endowed with spiritual gifts. They were not given to us so that we could feel good about ourselves, but as Paul explained in 1 Corinthians 12:7, *"But to each one is given the manifestation of the Spirit for the common good."* In other words, the body of Christ should benefit because of our presence. God gives each of us gifts, and He gives each of us opportunities to exercise those gifts within the body of Christ "for the common good" so that the whole body is benefited. We are called to minister to one another.

What is your attitude about your gifts and talents? Do you give yourself credit and pat yourself on the back for them, or do you give God glory and recognize Him as the source of any good in you? A right thinking about your gifts and talents ought to produce an attitude of humility and of gratefulness to God as the author of them.

Food for thought

God wants His body to be a community where instead of living selfishly, each of us uses our gifts and talents for the common good.

ACTS PRAYING

A - **ADORATION** - Take some time to praise God for who He is, identifying some of His attributes you find particularly meaningful.

C - **CONFESSION** - Remember, don't look for something to confess; that is introspection. Instead ask God to search your heart and to bring to mind anything that needs to be dealt with.

T - **THANKSGIVING** - Thank God for the many blessings of your life, taking a moment to ask God what you need to be thankful for.

S - **SUPPLICATION** - Pray for God's working in your life as you seek to assume your role in helping the body become the community God desires. Bring to Him any requests and needs that are on your heart.

Day 4: Have Fellowship With One Another

"...if we walk in the Light as He Himself is in the Light, we have fellowship with one another, and the blood of Jesus His Son cleanses us from all sin."

- 1 John 1:7

One of the consequences of being in right relationship with God is that we are pursuing right relationships with one another. Conversely, if we are not seeking to stay in fellowship with others in the body, we are not "walking in the Light" of Jesus. The word "fellowship" here is in the <u>present</u> tense in the original Greek. This means we are to maintain ongoing, continuous fellowship with one another. Either all is to be right in our relationships with one another, or we should be seeking to do what we can to make them right. Unfortunately, a lack of forgiveness is one of the main interrupters of Christian fellowship. Having just said "we are members of one another" (Eph. 4:25) Paul warns the Ephesians, "Be angry, and yet do not sin; do not let the sun go down on your anger, and do not give the devil an opportunity" (Ephesians 4:26-27). Unresolved conflict with one another gives an opportunity for the devil to have his way instead of Christ being exalted in our relationships. There will be conflict and even flashes of anger, but they must be dealt with quickly or else the devil will use the offense to divide the body. Throughout his life, the apostle John keeps reminding others of Jesus' "new commandment." In 1 John 3:11 he repeats, "For this is the message which you have heard from the beginning, that we should love one another." We are not loving one another if we neglect to deal with any interruption in the healthy fellowship the Lord wants us to have. God wants His body to be a community that works hard at working things out with each other.

In Matthew 5:23-24 Jesus addresses the correlation between our vertical relationship with God, and our horizontal relationships with one another. He instructs, "Therefore if you are presenting your offering at the altar, and there remember that your brother has something against you, leave your offering there before the altar and go; first be reconciled to your brother, and then come and present your offering." The implication is that someone is trying to atone for sins against their brother or sister by making offerings to God. Jesus makes it clear that the offering will mean nothing unless first things are made right with our brother or sister. If the "One Anothers" are defining our relationship with the body of Christ, then hindered fellowship with them is hindered fellowship with Him. Did you notice where the offense lies in this situation? Jesus says if "your brother has something against you", be reconciled. Not only must we forgive one another when we are offended, we must actively seek forgiveness from those we offend. Have you offended a brother or sister? The Old Testament law doesn't just address our relationship with God; it guides our relationships with one another. In Leviticus 19:11 we read, "You shall not steal, nor deal falsely, nor lie to one another." Have you offended with your business practices? "If you make a sale, moreover, to your friend or buy from your friend's hand, you shall not wrong one another" (Lev. 25:14). These horizontal dealings are spiritual matters. Leviticus 25:17 advises, "So you shall not wrong one another, but you shall fear your God; for I am the Lord your God." Offering marital advice, Peter admonishes, "You husbands in the same way, live with your wives in an understanding way, as with someone weaker, since she is a woman; and show her honor as a fellow heir of the grace of life, so that your prayers will not be hindered" (1 Peter 3:7). He literally refers to the wife as a "weaker vessel" – like a fine china cup that is easily damaged by mishandling. In the vernacular of Peter's culture, this is a more affirming view in contrast to the norm of disregarding a woman's feelings. If a husband offends his wife, even if it is unintentional, he must make things right or it will get in the way of his communion with God. Clearly, there is a correlation between our human relationships and our fellowship with God. We need to forgive one another, and we need to seek forgiveness from one another.

Food for thought

God wants His body to be a community that works hard at working things out with each other.

ACTS PRAYING

<u>A</u> - **ADORATION** - Take some time to praise God for who He is, identifying some of His attributes you find particularly meaningful. You may want to express your heart to Him in a journal.

<u>C</u> - **CONFESSION** - Remember, don't go looking for something to confess; that is introspection. Instead ask God to search your heart and to bring to mind anything that needs to be dealt with.

<u>T</u> - **THANKSGIVING** - Thank God for the many blessings of your life, taking a moment to ask God what you need to be thankful for.

<u>S</u> - **SUPPLICATION** - Pray for God to working in your life as you seek to assume your role in helping the body become the kind of community God desires. Bring to Him any requests and needs that are on your heart.

Day 5: Ministering Tolerance

"Therefore I, the prisoner of the Lord, implore you to walk in a manner worthy of the calling with which you have been called, with all humility and gentleness, with patience, showing tolerance for one another in love, being diligent to preserve the unity of the spirit in the bond of peace."

- Ephesians 4:1-3

Sin separates. It fractures human relationships. It gets in the way of loving my neighbor as myself. I may not be as conscious of some of my relationship sins because they are sins of omission instead of commission. Perhaps I have neglected relationships through selfishness or avoided them because of pride and unforgiveness. I may have sinned by what I didn't do instead of by what I did. Sin happens in our relationships when Christ is not in control.

In Ephesians 4:1-3 Paul reminds us of our responsibility to live consistently with what we profess to believe. At first glance, we may think that the call to "walk in a manner worthy" speaks of service, but these really are relationship verses. To "walk worthy" requires us to have humility and patience. It demands we "show tolerance to one another in love." The word "tolerance" means "to have patience with in regard to the errors or weaknesses of anyone." We learn here that we must preserve the "unity of the Spirit". Notice, we are not told to produce unity, but rather, to preserve it. Unity is natural when God's Spirit reigns in our hearts. We are exhorted to apply "diligence" to see that God's unity remains intact in His body. One of the unity interrupters is when we are offended by the errors or weaknesses of others and refuse to overlook them. Are you forbearing the faults of others?

Why is it that we sometimes find it hard to show tolerance to one another? Obviously there isn't one universal answer, nor is it adequate to answer simplistically by the general answer of sin.

Ironically, one barrier to tolerance is our own sense of justice. Let me explain. We expect people to do the right thing. Yet Scripture makes it clear that none of us always does the right thing. Psalm 14:3 says, "...there is no one who does good, not even one." In James 3:2 we are reminded, "...we all stumble in many ways." Solomon observed, "For a righteous man falls seven times, and rises again..." (Proverbs 24:16). We tend to focus on the fact that he rises, while forgetting that he also falls. Even righteous people stumble, and therefore we are in need of tolerance while we rise again. We want others to give us grace when we stumble, but is that what we do? When the failure of others affects us, do we consciously acknowledge that we are all human, or do we demand a perfection from others that we know we cannot attain? It requires "all humility [acknowledging our own imperfections] and gentleness, with patience" to be "showing tolerance for one another in love." Think about that last phrase, "in love." If we do not show tolerance – have patience with the errors or weaknesses of others – we are loving conditionally with performance-based love. God wants His church to be a community where everyone has the humility, patience, and love to show tolerance for the errors and weaknesses of each other. Do you want God to only love you when you perform rightly?

Food for thought

God wants His church to be a community where everyone has the humility, patience, and love to show tolerance for the errors and weaknesses of each other.

ACTS PRAYING

A - **ADORATION** - Take some time to praise God for who He is, identifying some of His attributes you find particularly meaningful.

C - **CONFESSION** - Remember, don't go looking for something to confess; that is introspection. Instead ask God to search your heart and to bring to mind anything that needs to be dealt with.

T - **THANKSGIVING** - Thank God for the many blessings of your life, taking a moment to ask God what you need to be thankful for.

S - **SUPPLICATION** - Pray for God's working in your life as you seek to assume your role in helping the body become the community God desires. Bring to Him any requests and needs that are on your heart.

WEEK THREE
"Bear One Another's Burdens"

Day 1: Bearing Burdens

"Bear one another's burdens, and thereby fulfill the law of Christ."
- Galatians 6:2

We are supposed to love one another in the community of Christ, and one of the ways we love is by bearing one another's burdens. Galatians 6 begins by saying, "...If anyone is caught in any trespass, you who are spiritual restore such a one in a spirit of gentleness..." (Galatians 6:1). We are to help each other bear the burden of sin. Genuine Christian fellowship, requires that we do not ignore sin, for as Matthew 18 points out, a sinning brother or sister must repent. But we must be quick to restore, however, when repentance is evident. We all stand before God only by grace. We who are so needy of grace must be quick to give it as well. This seems to be Paul's point in the last part of verse 1: "each one looking to yourself so that you too will not be tempted." The focus of this exhortation is not merely that we might sin in the same way, for this would be rare. The more common danger is that in recognizing another's sin, we might respond in a sinful manner such as pride, unforgiveness, or a lack of love. Paul seems to be continuing this point in verse 3: "If anyone thinks he is something when he is nothing, he deceives himself." We are all sinners before a holy God. Just because we might not sin in the same area as our brother or sister, or sin to the same degree, my sin put Jesus on the cross just as much as his or hers. Seeing another's stumbling affords no room for pride, for I am also "nothing" when it comes to holiness. James instructs us, "For whoever keeps the whole law and yet stumbles in one point, he has become guilty of all" (James 2:10). One sin is enough to make me a sinner who needs a Savior. That reality should prevent my thinking that I am superior to my brother or sister in need.

When we "Bear one another's burdens…" we "…fulfill the law of Christ." The early church referred to Christ's words, "You shall love your neighbor as yourself," as the "royal law" (James 2:8) or the "law of Christ." The word Paul uses for "burden" isn't just talking about any difficulty, but implies that which is beyond the normal load. While this obviously includes any burden of sin, it also includes material needs (e.g. financial burdens) as well as emotional burdens (excessive grief). Again we see that the Christian community is to have an "others" focus. Because we are one body, when one part is hurting the whole body is affected. When I see a brother or sister carrying an extra-heavy load, I must help. The first part of Galatians 6:4 adds: "But each one must examine his own work." It doesn't matter what others do; I only answer to God for doing my part. Someone else's failure to love does not remove my own responsibility. Verse 5 provides an important balance to this whole idea of bearing burdens. Paul states, "For each one will bear his own load." I must make certain that I do not become a burden to others by not doing what I can and should. The Greek word for "load" is different than the "burden" of verse 2. This word means "my normally allotted portion or responsibility." Each of us is to carry his or her load, but we are all to help carry the "burden" which goes beyond normal. Are you willing to minister to one another when the load becomes too great?

ONE ANOTHER

Food for thought

God wants His church to be a community where we bear each other's burdens as if they were our own.

ACTS PRAYING

A - **ADORATION** - Take some time to praise God for who He is, identifying some of His attributes you find particularly meaningful.

C - **CONFESSION** - Remember, don't go looking for something to confess; that is introspection. Instead ask God to search your heart and to bring to mind anything that needs to be dealt with.

T - **THANKSGIVING** - Thank God for the many blessings of your life, taking a moment to ask God what you need to be thankful for.

S - **SUPPLICATION** - Pray for God's working in your life as you seek to assume your role in helping the body become the community God desires. Bring to Him any requests and needs that are on your heart.

Day 2: Gathered in Fervent Prayer

"When Peter came to himself, he said, 'Now I know for sure that the Lord has sent forth His angel and rescued me from the hand of Herod and from all that the Jewish people were expecting.' And when he realized this, he went to the house of Mary, the mother of John who was also called Mark, where many were gathered together and were praying."

- Acts 12:11-12

The early church had little clout with the culture of their day. When society treated them with disrespect or disdain, they could organize no boycott or protest. When persecution arose, they had no army to defend themselves from harm. When the governing officials, sanctioned that persecution, they had no legislators or lobbyists to plead on their behalf. That does not indicate, however, that they were powerless. Through prayer, they could lay their concerns before Almighty God, and pray they did. As persecution heated up, so did their prayer meetings. At one point Herod the king arrested the apostle Peter with the intention of putting him to death. The church couldn't pull him out of jail, but they could pray him out. As Peter slept what was supposed to have been his last night on earth, "…prayer for him was being made fervently by the church to God" (Acts 12:5). In those pre-dawn hours, the Lord sent an angel who removed Peter's chains and escorted him unseen from the prison. At first Peter thought he was having a vision, but when the angel left him outside, he realized what had happened. When he came to Mary's house, he understood how – God's people were praying for him.

God has not changed, but have we? In this modern day do we have so many other options that we neglect fervent prayer? "We will only advance in our work as fast and as far as we advance on our knees. Prayer opens the channel between a soul and God; prayerlessness increases it. That is why prayer is so exhausting and so vital. If we believed it, the prayer meeting would be as full as the church" (Alan Redpath). But our prayer meetings aren't full. Perhaps it is because we are not aware of our brother or sister's need as we should be, or maybe it is because we don't believe God is willing and able to intervene. Jim Elliot was eventually martyred as he attempted to take the gospel to an Ecuadorian tribe. He said this about the prayers of others on his behalf: "I have felt the impact of your prayer in these past weeks. I am certain now that nothing has more powerful influence on this life of mine than your prayers." Could he have laid his life on the altar without the prayer support of others? But we do not pray as we should, in part, because we do not care about other's circumstances as we should. It may be that we <u>need</u> others to pray for us in this area of our concern for and connection with each other. Paul prayed this for the Thessalonians: "may the Lord cause you to increase and abound in love for one another" (1 Thessalonians 3:12).

Perhaps the reason we do not pray as we should is not from lack of concern or lack of faith in God's ability, but from a lack of confidence in our own prayers. However feeble, our prayers are powerful because God to whom we pray is powerful. We may not fully see the effect of our prayers this side of heaven, but I suspect there will be plenty of encouragement there as we look back on our prayers here. Edith Schaeffer wrote, "…we all have to wait until the astonishing discoveries will one day be made, and find out whose faithful prayer in hospitals, prisons, jungles, wheelchairs, crowded city apartments, cabins in the woods, farms, factories or concentration camps has been a part of a specific victory in snatching someone from a circle of death, or in breaking chains so that there seems to be an ease for that one in stepping into new life. I feel sure that we'll be surprised beyond measure to discover who or how many will receive the rewards for their part in taking literally and with simple faith and trust the responsibility to intercede, to pray, to make requests day in and day out."

Food for thought

God wants His body to be a community that fervently prays for one another.

ACTS PRAYING

A - **ADORATION** - Take some time to praise God for who He is, identifying some of His attributes you find particularly meaningful.

C - **CONFESSION** - Remember, don't go looking for something to confess; that is introspection. Instead ask God to search your heart and to bring to mind anything that needs to be dealt with.

T - **THANKSGIVING** - Thank God for the many blessings of your life, taking a moment to ask God what you need to be thankful for.

S - **SUPPLICATION** - Pray for God's working in your life as you seek to assume your role in helping the body become the community God desires. Bring to Him any requests and needs that are on your heart.

Day 3: Giving The Comfort We Receive

"Blessed be the God and Father of our Lord Jesus Christ, the Father of mercies and God of all comfort, who comforts us in all our affliction so that we will be able to comfort those who are in any affliction with the comfort with which we ourselves are comforted by God."

- 2 Corinthians 1:3-4

No matter how secure our environment or comfortable our situation, there are no immunization shots that protect us from trials. Each of us will encounter life head-on with all its difficulties. Contrary to the teaching of some, Christianity is not the "bridge over troubled water." Jesus said, "In the world you will have tribulation" (John 16:33), and He said that so the disciples wouldn't be surprised when it happened. **The joy of Christianity is not the absence of difficulties but the presence of God**. Jesus continues by saying "... but take courage, I have overcome the world."

What a joy in the midst of any distress to know the "Father of mercies and God of all comfort." As the Psalmist said, "I will fear no evil, for **You** are with me." It is during the difficult times that we are most keenly aware of the "with-ness" of God, and as we turn to Him we experience His comfort in all our afflictions. The reason is because of His great love and compassion for us - after all, He is the "Father of mercies."

Not only is God's comfort abundant in all our afflictions, but there is a second blessing as well. **With every gift of God's comfort we receive, a door of ministry is opened up to us**. He comforts us so that we may be comforted, but also so that we may be ministers of that comfort to those who are in any affliction with God's comfort. As we experience the comfort and power of God, He will lead us to others who need to experience that. Maybe they are going through a similar circumstance and need to hear what God has done for another. Or even if we haven't gone through the same experience and don't know how to comfort them, we know He can - "The Father of mercies and God of all comfort."

Food for thought

God wants His church to be a community where we not only are ministered to, but where we minister the comfort we have received.

ACTS PRAYING

A - ADORATION - This passage tells us that the God who has blessed us with comfort Himself deserves to be blessed (to adore and thank Him for all the benefits). Take some time to do this in your letter to Him.

C - CONFESSION – Don't go looking for something to confess; just ask God to bring to mind anything that needs to be dealt with.

T - THANKSGIVING - Thank God for His supernatural comfort in the midst of our circumstances. Thank Him for comfort you have received in the past, and by faith thank Him for comfort you presently need.

S - SUPPLICATION - Pray for those you know who need God's comfort and for Him to lead you to those who you can comfort from what God has done for you.

Day 4: Accepting the Messes of Burden-Bearing Relationships

"Where no oxen are, the manger is clean, but much revenue comes by the strength of the ox."

- Proverbs 14:4

I am sure many would look at this verse and wonder what it has to do with anything relevant to them. We are talking about bearing one another's burdens, and while oxen are associated with burden-bearing, what has that to do with us? Hidden in this obscure nugget of proverbial wisdom is a powerful principle that applies to many different areas of our walk with God and His people. Try to think with me through the lens of one involved in agriculture. The farmer who has no oxen in his or her stable has no manure to clean up, but has no milk either. When this one needs to plow the fields or haul a heavy burden, they must carry it alone. **If we want the increase the ox offers, we must accept the problems and responsibilities that come with that.**

When we examine the principle Solomon puts forward in this proverb, the parallel to other areas of life is striking. All too often, we choose the path of least resistance. We seek to avoid pain and problems, yet in the process we rob ourselves of opportunities for growth and benefit. The old locker room adage, "no pain, no gain", holds true to more than just weight lifting. It holds true to life. If we choose not to open up and share ourselves with others, we don't experience the pain and problems and messes a relationship can bring, but we also don't experience the joys and growth and ministry that can happen.

Many times we "purchase our oxen" figuratively speaking – be it entering into a relationship with someone for ministry or making a commitment to help – and naively expect that there will be no problems with it. When the problems or difficulties come (as they always do) we balk as if something were terribly wrong. Sometimes we bail out when we shouldn't all because we didn't like the smell of manure or didn't know how to use a shovel. In the process, we rob ourselves and others of the much "revenue" (increase and benefit) that comes by the strength of the ox.

Food for thought

God wants His body to be a community that doesn't allow the messiness of ministry to keep us from being there for one another.

ACTS PRAYING

A - **ADORATION** - Take some time to praise God for who He is, identifying some of His attributes you find particularly meaningful.

C - **CONFESSION** - Remember, don't go looking for something to confess; that is introspection. Instead ask God to search your heart and to bring to mind anything that needs to be dealt with.

T - **THANKSGIVING** - Thank God for the many blessings of your life, taking a moment to ask God what you need to be thankful for.

S - **SUPPLICATION** - Pray for God's working in your life as you seek to assume your role in helping the body become the community God desires. Bring to Him any requests and needs that are on your heart.

Day 5: We Need "We"

"Make every effort to come to me soon; for Demas, having loved this present world, has deserted me and gone to Thessalonica; Crescens has gone to Galatia, Titus to Dalmatia. Only Luke is with me. Pick up Mark and bring him with you, for he is useful to me for service. But Tychicus I have sent to Ephesus. When you come bring the cloak which I left at Troas with Carpus, and the books, especially the parchments."

– 2 Timothy 4:9-13

Near the end of the Apostle Paul's life he writes his last epistle that is part of our New Testament. He is in the Mamertine prison at Rome as he pens his second letter to his disciple, Timothy. The sentence of death has been decreed by Nero, and the end is near. Faced with such a reality, one can both sense and understand the urgency in his voice. The people he refers in these verses are mostly familiar ones – Timothy, Demas, Crescens, Titus, Luke, Mark, and Tychicus – but it is in their back-story that we gain one of the clearest glimpses of Paul's humanity. Some of these relationships span decades. Do you have such people in your life? Ones who know you and your history well? Hidden behind these names are profound principles about bearing each other's burdens. Let me share the life lessons from these verses than not only apply to Paul and his companions, but to each of us as well.

The name Demas doesn't appear in a very positive light here: "…having loved this present world…has deserted me." Wouldn't you hate for your name to be listed in the permanent record of Scripture in such a way? In Philemon, Paul mentions him as a fellow-worker, and he is also referenced in the book of Colossians as a companion. Here, he is called a deserter. The lure of this world was too much. This record stands as a stark reminder than we never graduate from spiritual danger. His danger was worldliness, what is yours?

Next Paul identifies Luke – literally, stating "Luke alone is still with me." This partnership goes back decades. It is worth reflecting on what Luke could have been doing instead of hanging out with his imprisoned friend. He was a trained doctor. By all indications, he was quite well educated. We know he was an historian. There are lots of other things he could have been doing, but being there for Paul and helping bear his burdens was at the top of Luke's list. He leveraged his gifts for God's kingdom instead of his own. His mention reminds us that we never graduate from spiritual usefulness.

Crescens is perhaps not as familiar to us, but Titus we know well from the epistle which bears his name and the many references to him in others of Paul's letters. Tychicus is introduced in Acts 20 on Paul's journey to Jerusalem which leads to his first arrest. Paul often refers to him as "the beloved brother." Another faithful burden-bearer, Paul relies on him to run errands and deliver messages (e.g. Ephesians 6:21, Colossians 4:7, Titus 3:12). The mention of his being sent to Ephesus here leads us to infer that not only is he delivering this epistle to Timothy, but is making himself available to cover responsibilities so Timothy can be free to visit Paul.

The request of Mark is particularly poignant when one remembers the sharp division of Acts 15. When Mark bailed out on the first missionary journey, Paul essentially wrote him off as useless. So disgusted was Paul with Mark's fickleness that when Barnabas wanted to bring him along on the second missionary journey, it caused the breakup of this important ministry duo. Here at the end of his life, Paul says, "Pick up Mark and bring him with you, for he is **useful** to me for service." One can only imagine how much this simple request meant to Mark. He would go one to be a faithful disciple to Peter and write one of the Gospels. His addition here reminds us that we never graduate from forgiving and forgiveness.

The personal pronouns are worth noting here. Six times Paul refers to himself. Look what he asks for: He writes, come to me soon (v.9), bring Mark (v.11), bring my cloak that I left at Troas, and bring my books and parchments (v.13). Sometimes we read the Scriptures and if we aren't careful we spiritualize them to the point that we don't think about what they mean practically. What is Paul really saying here? He is sending the message that "I'm lonely, I'm cold, and I'm bored." Without stating it explicitly, he is declaring loudly, "I'm human!" The principle can and should be personally applied by each of us. This side of heaven, we will never graduate from humanness. This is why we need to harness the power of WE. The important message of this whole devotional drives home how much we should value the community of believers. Do you? Does your life and engagement with your local assembly reflect that value appropriately?

Food for thought

God wants His body to be a community that understands how much we need one another, and reflects that value with how we engage each other.

ACTS PRAYING

A - **ADORATION** - Take some time to praise God for who He is, identifying some of His attributes you find particularly meaningful.

C - **CONFESSION** - Remember, don't go looking for something to confess; that is introspection. Instead ask God to search your heart and to bring to mind anything that needs to be dealt with.

T - **THANKSGIVING** - Thank God for the many blessings of your life, taking a moment to ask God what you need to be thankful for.

S - **SUPPLICATION** - Pray for God's working in your life as you seek to assume your role in helping the body become the community God desires. Bring to Him any requests and needs that are on your heart.

WEEK FOUR
"Encourage One Another"

Day 1: Building Each Other Up

"Therefore encourage one another and build up one another, just as you also are doing."

- 1 Thessalonians 5:11

Most churches and even most lives are woefully deficient in vitamin E – encouragement. In today's theme verse Paul challenges the Thessalonians to encourage one another and to build up one another. Both of these are "present imperatives" in the Greek. That means they are commands to do something continuously. The word "encourage" (*parakaleo*) literally means "to call alongside." God wants us to walk alongside each other and speak words that "build up." The phrase "build up" is from a Greek word (*oikodomeo*) that refers to a building under construction. Each of us is an unfinished project. We are in process, and God wants us to come alongside each other as a help to that process. We are all appreciative when someone speaks an encouraging word in the midst of a hard task. Work is easier when done with another. People feature prominently in motivating us to do what we ought. That is where the two exhortations go hand in hand. We need to come alongside each other to encourage, and when we do, we should build each other up. Paul's challenge is all the more intriguing because he follows by saying the Thessalonians are already doing what he desires. Even those who are already encouraging and building others up need to be encouraged to encourage. God wants His church to be a community that is in the building-people-up business, not tearing people down.

Unfortunately, it is characteristic of fallen human nature to criticize more than to encourage. There are even more negative words for emotions in our vocabulary than positive ones. Penn State linguistics professor Robert Schrauf researched the vocabularies of two different age groups in two different languages and cultures and found this surprising result: "Half of all the words that people produce from their working vocabulary to express emotion are negative…30% are positive and 20% are neutral. And every single one of these groups, young Mexicans and old Mexicans, young Anglos and old Anglos, had the same proportions."[3] It seems everyone has more experience and capacity with the negative than the positive. That isn't good news. Child development experts at the University of Kansas found a direct correlation between encouragement and I.Q. They found that the children with the highest IQ's (an average of 117), not only heard more from their parents, but most of what they heard was positive (86% encouragements vs. 14% discouragements). The children on the low end of the scale (an average IQ of 79) heard far more negatives (27% encouragements vs. 73% discouragements). Psychologist John Gottman tried to predict whether a couple would stay together or divorce based on the ratio of positive-to-negative comments he observed as they interacted for fifteen minutes. Healthy relationships averaged at least five encouragements for every criticism. He predicted those with less than a 1/1 ration would divorce. Ten years later 94% of them had.[4] The same principles turned out to be an amazingly accurate predictor of job performance as well. It seems we all need encouragement if we are to succeed. God wants us to speak encouragement to one another.

---

[3] ABC News, Feb. 2, 2005.
[4] http://en.wikipedia.org/wiki/Positivity/negativity_ratio

Food for thought

God wants His church to be a community that is in the "building-people-up" business, not tearing people down.

ACTS PRAYING

A - **ADORATION** - Take some time to praise God for who He is, identifying some of His attributes you find particularly meaningful. You may want to express your heart to Him in a journal.

C - **CONFESSION** - Remember, don't go looking for something to confess; that is introspection. Instead ask God to search your heart and to bring to mind anything that needs to be dealt with.

T - **THANKSGIVING** - Thank God for the many blessings of your life, taking a moment to ask God what you need to be thankful for.

S - **SUPPLICATION** - Pray for God to working in your life as you seek to assume your role in helping the body become the kind of community God desires. Bring to Him any requests and needs that are on your heart.

Day 2: Speaking Encouragement

"…be filled with the Spirit, speaking to one another in psalms and hymns and spiritual songs, singing and making melody with your heart to the Lord."

- Ephesians 5:18-19

The apostle Paul instructs us to be "filled" with the Spirit of God. This doesn't mean that we get more of God's Spirit; rather, it means the Spirit is getting more of us. We are commanded to allow God's Spirit, who already indwells every true Christian, to fill every area of our lives. If Christ is on the throne of our hearts, all our human relationships will be affected in a positive way. We will speak in healthy ways, instead of tearing each other down. If we are Spirit-filled, we _will_ speak to one another. We will have something to say and the freedom to say it. This probably includes both speaking in the sense of teaching, as well as casually in regular interaction with other believers. The content of our conversation with others will be both mutually edifying and glorifying to God. We are to speak to one another in "psalms" and "hymns" and "spiritual songs". As you probably guessed, psalms refer to the poetic books of the Old Testament bearing that name. This is a collection of 150 songs written by different leaders of the Old Testament era. Hymns are not as straightforward. These are not the songs in your church hymnal – those are all written within the last few hundred years. The word simply means songs of praise. While psalms are songs <u>about</u> a request for deliverance or celebrating God's intervention, hymns are songs of praise <u>to</u> God not for what He does, but for who He is. Spiritual songs are literally spiritual odes. The "ode" was a classical Greek method of storytelling somewhat like the modern ballad. Paul qualifies this with the adjective "spiritual."

What in the world does it mean to speak to one another in such a way? Is all of life supposed to be like a Broadway play, with every major turn of events interrupted by a show-stopping musical number? No, Paul says "speaking to one another", not "singing to one another." The next phrase gives helpful clarity: "singing and making melody with your heart to the Lord." Our singing is to the Lord. Don't get so focused on the method used that you miss the attitude. We only have a song in our heart when we are joyful. The phrase "making melody" refers to musical accompaniment – it gives the idea of an instrument playing notes and tones compatible with the overall song. Think about that. Like musicians following the conductor, what we say to one another should be in sync with the director's wishes. It should not be discordant. God wants His church to be a community whose hearts are in such harmony with Him that our speech to each other is in harmony with His plan. The Apostle Peter conveys a similar thought in 1 Peter 4:11 – "Whoever speaks, is to do so as one who is speaking the utterances of God". God wants to so pervade our lives that in our relationships with one another we say what He would say in every situation. Think of what kind of community the church will be if that is true all the time. We can't control what others will do; we can't even control ourselves. If, however, we walk in yieldedness to Christ – if He is in control of every area of our lives – He will be in control of our tongues. We <u>will</u> say what He wants said.

Food for thought

God wants His church to be a community whose hearts are in so in harmony with Him that our speech to each other is in harmony with His plan.

ACTS PRAYING

A - **ADORATION** - Take some time to praise God for who He is, identifying some of His attributes you find particularly meaningful. You may want to express your heart to Him in a journal.

C - **CONFESSION** - Remember, don't go looking for something to confess; that is introspection. Instead ask God to search your heart and to bring to mind anything that needs to be dealt with.

T - **THANKSGIVING** - Thank God for the many blessings of your life, taking a moment to ask God what you need to be thankful for.

S - **SUPPLICATION** - Pray for God to working in your life as you seek to assume your role in helping the body become the kind of community God desires. Bring to Him any requests and needs that are on your heart.

Day 3: The Danger of Not Encouraging

"But encourage one another day after day, as long as it is still called 'Today,' so that none of you will be hardened by the deceitfulness of sin."

- Hebrews 3:13

One of the enemy's greatest tools is discouragement. He knows that if he can discourage us, even if he can't stop us, he can at least slow us down. But God has designed the body so that we have the right, ability, and responsibility to help each other avoid discouragement. Ecclesiastes 4:9-10 tells us, "Two are better than one because they have a good return for their labor, for if either of them falls, the one will lift up his companion. But woe to the one who falls when there is not another to lift him up." God wants His body to be a community where discouragement is in danger of extinction. He wants us so connected to each other that there is always another to lift us up and encourage us when we fall prey to the enemy's darts of discouragement. What are we to do? We are to "encourage one another" – to come along side each other. Who are we to encourage? Don't miss the obvious here – we are to encourage "one another." Encouragement is a two-way street. We should be giving it _and_ receiving it. If you are feeling the need for encouragement, you may find it easy to overlook that someone around you needs it too. Maybe they won't be able to reciprocate right away, but your gift of encouragement when they need it will be repaid many times. You can encourage others in trust that in God's time He will send someone to encourage you as well. In the meantime, it may help to get your eyes off yourself.

How often are we to encourage one another? We are to encourage "day after day." This call from the writer of Hebrews is a "present tense imperative" in the Greek – a command to do something continuously. We all need encouragement every day, so we should give it every day. When are we to encourage? The author tells us, "as long as it is still called 'Today'." If we are sensitive to the Lord, He will prompt us concerning those who need to be encouraged. Unfortunately, it is all too easy to put off obedience to a task as intangible as encouraging. But the verse tells us we need to act on these promptings while it is still called "Today." Paul challenges the Ephesians to not let the sun go down on their anger, so they might not "give the devil an opportunity" (Ephesians 4:27). We should also not let the sun go down on any prompting to encourage someone for the same reason. Why are we to encourage one another? We need to encourage, because without it, any of us can be "hardened by the deceitfulness of sin." There is an interesting reference in the immediate context of today's verse. Hebrews 3:8 reads, "Do not harden your hearts as when they provoked Me, in the day of trial in the wilderness." Since there is a "day of trial" (temptation), we dare not delay our encouragement to another day or we may be too late. God may want to use us this day to keep another from hardening their hearts toward Him. If so, it is both a privilege and a responsibility. Jeremiah writes, "The heart is more deceitful than all else and is desperately sick" (Jer. 17:9). Our hearts can become hardened toward God by the deceitfulness of our sinful propensities. In our moments of weakness we need those around us to love us enough to come alongside. In someone else's moment of need, we may be the person God uses to come alongside them.

Food for thought

God wants His church to be a community where discouragement is in danger of extinction.

ACTS PRAYING

A - **ADORATION** - Take some time to praise God for who He is, identifying some of His attributes you find particularly meaningful. You may want to express your heart to Him in a journal.

C - **CONFESSION** - Remember, don't go looking for something to confess; that is introspection. Instead ask God to search your heart and to bring to mind anything that needs to be dealt with.

T - **THANKSGIVING** - Thank God for the many blessings of your life, taking a moment to ask God what you need to be thankful for.

S - **SUPPLICATION** - Pray for God to working in your life as you seek to assume your role in helping the body become the kind of community God desires. Bring to Him any requests and needs that are on your heart.

Day 4: Physical Encouragement

"Greet one another with a kiss of love. Peace be to you all who are in Christ."

- 1 Peter 5:14

You have surely come across the exhortation to "Greet one another with a kiss" as you read your Bible. In addition to here in 1 Peter, it appears in Romans 16:16, 1 Corinthians 16:20, 2 Corinthians 13:12, and 1 Thessalonians 5:26. We are told in Acts 20:37 that on their final parting, the Ephesian elders "began to weep aloud and embraced Paul, and repeatedly kissed him." It is a normal and natural part of Biblical culture to greet one another physically with a kiss. The Old Testament is full of examples dating back to ancient times of such a greeting being shared between parents and children, between siblings, and between friends. It is primarily reserved for members of the same sex. Solomon writes, "He kisses the lips who gives a right answer" (Proverbs 24:26). As you probably already assume, this is not referring to a romantic or sensual kiss. The word "love" here is *agape* – selfless, unconditional, committed love. Many of the Biblical passages that reference this practice include the adjective "holy", making clear that there is nothing inappropriate associated with the action. The purpose behind this cultural practice is to encourage and express an affectionate commitment to each other. This reality must make it all the more painful when Judas chooses this method to betray our Lord. Proverbs 27: 6 states, "deceitful are the kisses of an enemy." The devil loves to pervert what God intends to be a good thing.

Have you ever wondered why this practice isn't common in churches today? While we may not kiss each other, we do still practice physical encouragement. We shake hands. We give each other hugs. We pat each other on the back. But perhaps we never stop to think about how important <u>and how Biblical</u> such practices are. The idea appears often enough in Scripture that it cannot be overlooked. God wants

His church to be a community that expresses a holy affection for one another. Communication is far more than mere words. There are some things that can only be communicated by actions. The Biblical frequency of such practices seems to underscore that we all need to be touched. For some, church may be the only place anyone ever offers such encouragement. Our Lord modeled physical and non-verbal encouragement when He wept. He often used touch to heal.

Perhaps the most memorable example of physical and non-verbal encouragement is when He washed the disciples' feet in the Upper Room. This was not mere symbolism. In a dusty culture where you walked nearly everywhere, dirty feet were the norm, and the need for them to be washed was universal. Jesus knelt at the feet of His followers, bathed their feet in a basin, and then gently wiped them with a towel. It was an everyday occurrence, and the practice probably felt good to path-worn feet. The only thing unusual about the story is who is washing the feet. Jesus, the leader, is taking the role normally reserved for a servant. He is making the point that it is right and appropriate to serve one another even in physical ways. In John 13:14 He instructs the disciples, "If I then, the Lord and the Teacher, washed your feet, you also ought to wash one another's feet." Maybe foot-washing seems strange today because it doesn't fill the same practical purpose, but there are physical ways we can encourage each other without saying a word. Today, look for an opportunity to reach out and touch someone. It is sure to encourage!

Food for thought

God wants His body to be a community that expresses a holy affection for one another.

ACTS PRAYING

A - **ADORATION** - Take some time to praise God for who He is, identifying some of His attributes you find particularly meaningful. You may want to express your heart to Him in a journal.

C - **CONFESSION** - Remember, don't go looking for something to confess; that is introspection. Instead ask God to search your heart and to bring to mind anything that needs to be dealt with.

T - **THANKSGIVING** - Thank God for the many blessings of your life, taking a moment to ask God what you need to be thankful for.

S - **SUPPLICATION** - Pray for God to working in your life as you seek to assume your role in helping the body become the kind of community God desires. Bring to Him any requests and needs that are on your heart.

Day 5: An Assembly of Encouragement

"...and let us consider how to stimulate one another to love and good deeds, not forsaking our own assembling together, as is the habit of some, but encouraging one another; and all the more as you see the day drawing near."

- Hebrews 10:24-25

As we consider the last "One Another" commands, bring to a close our look at the kind of community God wants His church to be. Just prior to verse 24, the author of Hebrews exhorts believers to draw near to Christ, and in the same breath, he calls us to draw near to each other – "not forsaking our own assembling together." When you place several flaming logs together, you have a bonfire, but if you take one of these logs and set it off to itself, the fire quickly dwindles. As the body of Christ, we need each other, and we need regular times together. Hebrews calls us to a lifestyle of "encouraging one another." The Greek word translated "forsaking" means "to desert or leave behind." Hebrews 13:5 employs this exact word, quoting Christ who says, "I will never desert you, nor will I ever forsake you." He will never forsake us, but when we forsake assembling with the members of His body, we are forsaking Him. Apparently this was a problem as evidenced by the phrase, "as is the habit of some." There will certainly be occasions when we are unable to meet with our fellow brethren because of illness or travel; that is not the concern here. The word for "habit" (*ethos*) has to do with our ongoing character. For some, meeting together with their fellow Christians simply isn't viewed as all that important. It is important to the Lord however, and it is needful for all of us. Each of us needs the encouragement, equipping and accountability we get from others when we come together. We also have a responsibility to impart those same realities into the lives of others.

What is it to look like when the body of Christ assembles? This passage paints a portrait of a church where each one is committed to being involved. Assembling together is not neglected. Our participation isn't simply to begin when we arrive either. We are instructed to "consider how to stimulate one another to love and good deeds." The word "consider" (*katanoeo*) means to contemplate. It speaks of forethought and intentionality. We need to plan ways to move one another toward expressions of love and acts of goodness. When you think about it, love and good deeds pretty much covers all of the "One Another" commands. Did you notice where the responsibility for action resides? According to the writer of Hebrews, we are all to "stimulate one another." Are we tempted to skip church because we don't feel like going or think we won't get anything out of it? We need to recognize that it is not our participation as a spectator that is needed, for that will probably not be missed. What is missed if we forsake the assembly is the ministry God wants us to contribute.

Ministry is not merely the responsibility of the clergy. Christianity was never intended to be a spectator sport. We are all to be ministers to one another. That is why the Bible gives so many different "One Another" instructions to all of us. Instead of changing churches because no one seems to be ministering to us, perhaps we need to be the ones changing the church into a place where we own the responsibility to be "encouraging one another." We need to have the attitude that if we aren't there, someone else might not be stimulated toward love and good deeds as they ought to be. God wants His church to be a community where each one comes together with a plan to encourage someone else toward love and good deeds. How important is it for the church to operate this way? It is not a need that diminishes. Encouraging one another becomes more and more important as each day passes. You need to take it as a personal responsibility to minister encouragement "all the more as you see the day drawing near." The closer we get to Christ's return, the greater the need we all have for encouragement. Start today thinking up ways you can stimulate others to do the same.

Food for thought

God wants His church to be a community where each one comes together with a plan to encourage someone else toward love and good deeds.

ACTS PRAYING

A - **ADORATION** - Take some time to praise God for who He is, identifying some of His attributes you find particularly meaningful. You may want to express your heart to Him in a journal.

C - **CONFESSION** - Remember, don't go looking for something to confess; that is introspection. Instead ask God to search your heart and to bring to mind anything that needs to be dealt with.

T - **THANKSGIVING** - Thank God for the many blessings of your life, taking a moment to ask God what you need to be thankful for.

S - **SUPPLICATION** - Pray for God to working in your life as you seek to assume your role in helping the body become the kind of community God desires. Bring to Him any requests and needs that are on your heart.

WEEK FIVE
"Be Accountable to One Another"

Day 1: The Encouragement of Humility and Accountability

"You younger men, likewise, be subject to your elders; and all of you, clothe yourselves with humility toward one another, for God is opposed to the proud, but gives grace to the humble."

- 1 Peter 5:5

"God is opposed to the proud," and the rest of us don't like them very much either. No one enjoys being around people who are full of themselves. On the flip side though, there is something inherently attractive and encouraging about humility. Peter exhorts each of us to "clothe yourselves with humility toward one another." The Greek word translated "clothe yourselves" is sometimes used of a slave who ties on an apron. We are meant to wear humility like a garment, and fasten it tight so it doesn't come off. This attribute is even more desirable in someone who serves as a spiritual leader, and is equally appropriate. Paul exhorts us in Philippians 2:5 us to "…have this attitude in yourselves which was also in Christ Jesus", and then goes on to describe its parameters with phrases like "emptied Himself", "taking the form of a bond-servant", and "He humbled Himself." If Christ clothed Himself with humility, it drives home how inappropriate it is for any of us to be clothed with pride. In the Mosaic Law, God instructs Israel, "you shall not rule with severity over one another" (Leviticus 25:46). Even if we are placed as a leader over another, we should exercise that role with humility. In the same context as our day's verse, Peter exhorts leaders to: "be examples to the flock" (1 Peter 5:3). If we all are to clothe ourselves with humility, leaders ought to take the lead in this. Each of us encourages others toward humility when we exhibit it ourselves.

Paul instructs the Ephesians, "and be subject to one another in the fear of Christ" (Ephesians 5:21). All of us are to make ourselves accountable to each other. In the body of Christ, no one is above accountability. When we voluntarily place ourselves in subjection to each other, we encourage the same behavior in others. The verse also implies that mutual subjection is an obligation that comes with being Christ's body. What does the encouragement of humility and mutual accountability look like practically? Paul gives one example in 1 Corinthians 11:33 – "So then, my brethren, when you come together to eat, wait for one another." The context is their observance of the Lord's Supper. In Paul's day, it is taken as an entire meal like its Old Testament counterpart, the Passover Seder. In their selfishness and greed, the Corinthians are turning the Lord's Supper into a fight to see who can fill their plates first. Some are gorging themselves while others go away hungry. One simple way we can express humility and mutual accountability is to put the other person first. In Philippians 2:3-4 Paul exhorts, "Do nothing from selfishness or empty conceit, but with humility of mind regard one another as more important than yourselves; do not merely look out for your own personal interests, but also for the interests of others." Everyone is encouraged when we live this way. The problem is that humility isn't merely an action; it is a heart attitude. We cannot fake humility. Either it is real, or its absence is really obvious. When we do observe genuine humility in someone else, we see what the body of Christ is meant to be: a community where each of us puts one another before ourselves. Maybe that is why humility has such a great potential for encouraging one another.

Food for thought

God wants His body to be a community where each of us puts one another before ourselves.

ACTS PRAYING

A - **ADORATION** - Take some time to praise God for who He is, identifying some of His attributes you find particularly meaningful. You may want to express your heart to Him in a journal.

C - **CONFESSION** - Remember, don't go looking for something to confess; that is introspection. Instead ask God to search your heart and to bring to mind anything that needs to be dealt with.

T - **THANKSGIVING** - Thank God for the many blessings of your life, taking a moment to ask God what you need to be thankful for.

S - **SUPPLICATION** - Pray for God to working in your life as you seek to assume your role in helping the body become the kind of community God desires. Bring to Him any requests and needs that are on your heart.

Day 2: Encouraging One Another With Truth

"Let the word of Christ richly dwell within you, with all wisdom teaching and admonishing one another with psalms and hymns and spiritual songs, singing with thankfulness in your hearts to God."

- Colossians 3:16

As you read this verse, you probably notice how similar it is to the thought Paul conveys in Ephesians 5:19. One of the ways we can align our speech with God's will and purpose is if we are letting "the word of Christ richly dwell within" us. The phrase "richly dwell" is and imperative (command) and is the main verb in this sentence. The more we are under the influence of the word of God, the more we speak in line with what He has to say. As with the Ephesians passage, Paul paints a picture of Christians as members of a great orchestra playing constantly on beat with the conductor. When we do this we are able to teach and admonish one another God's way. The word "teaching" means simply "to instruct by word of mouth." When we are under the influence of God's word and in harmony with the conductor, we are able to speak into the lives of others in a way that equips and gives direction. The word "admonishing" literally means "to place before the mind." It carries the idea of warning or exhorting. While we cannot control how others will receive our admonishing, we <u>will</u> speak truth when led by the conductor.

Comparing this verse to Ephesians 5:19, you notice that here Paul substitutes "thankfulness" for the phrase "making melody" of Ephesians. Paul also says in Colossians 3:17, "Whatever you do in word or deed, do all in the name of the Lord Jesus, giving thanks through Him to the Father." While "thankfulness" and "giving thanks" seem repetitious in the English translation, they are two different Greek words in the original text. The latter phrase (*eucharisteo*) more closely aligns with what we understand as giving thanks. Verse 16 actually uses the Greek word *charis* which normally is translated "grace." It fact, the same word *is* translated "grace" in Colossians 4:5 – "Let your speech always be with grace." The literal meaning should not be missed here. Our speaking to one another should manifest grace, and certainly if we admonish another we should be mindful of God's grace, lest we be stained by pride. We admonish another for their good, not because of our own superiority. God wants His church to be a community that speaks truth with grace.

Not only is our speaking to one another to be influenced by the word of God, it *is* to be the word of God. Paul closes out the fourth chapter of 1 Thessalonians, saying "Therefore comfort one another with these words" (1 Thessalonians 4:18). Under the inspiration of the Holy Spirit, Paul began this thought back in verse 13 with the explanation: "...we do not want you to be uninformed, brethren, about those who are asleep, so that you will not grieve as do the rest that have no hope." Paul teaches these believers about the Second Coming of Christ and the glorious future that awaits all who know Him. This truth has to be a great comfort to any Christians in Thessalonica who are grieving the death of some beloved family member. While none of us can write Scripture today, we *can* speak it to one another to provide comfort and perspective on life. Truth always builds up even if it isn't what we want to hear. It especially builds up when it gives us a godly perspective on the circumstances going on in our lives. God wants us to encourage one another with truth. Who can you encourage today?

Food for thought

God wants His church to be a community that speaks truth with grace to comfort and encourage one other.

ACTS PRAYING

A - **ADORATION** - Take some time to praise God for who He is, identifying some of His attributes you find particularly meaningful. You may want to express your heart to Him in a journal.

C - **CONFESSION** - Remember, don't go looking for something to confess; that is introspection. Instead ask God to search your heart and to bring to mind anything that needs to be dealt with.

T - **THANKSGIVING** - Thank God for the many blessings of your life, taking a moment to ask God what you need to be thankful for.

S - **SUPPLICATION** - Pray for God to working in your life as you seek to assume your role in helping the body become the kind of community God desires. Bring to Him any requests and needs that are on your heart.

Day 3: Be at Peace With One Another

"Salt is good; but if the salt becomes unsalty, with what will you make it salty again? Have salt in yourselves, and be at peace with one another."

- Mark 9:50

Jesus calls us to "be at peace with one another." To be at peace means to have no friction between two individuals or to have no irritant causing conflict. God wants His church to be a community of peacemakers, especially with one another. If the Prince of Peace rules in our hearts, we will pursue peace with each other. We have a beautiful picture of peace in Noah's rainbow—the visible sign of the promise God would never flood the earth again. It was a picture of peace for Noah and his family, a picture of judgment past and a new beginning full of the promises of God. That can be true in our lives as well. Jesus bore our judgment on the Cross. That judgment is past and in His resurrection Life we have the promise of a new beginning and a walk of peace with Him every day. It also speaks of the harmony that we can know with one another. Think of the rainbow again. Not only is the rainbow a symbol of God's promise to never flood the earth again, it is a colorful picture of peace and harmony, the colors of the rainbow blending into a beautiful work of art. That is what God desires our lives to look like, a picture of harmony with others.

The Prophet Zechariah instructs, "speak the truth to one another; judge with truth and judgment for peace in your gates" (Zechariah 8:16). Paul exhorts the Thessalonians, "…live in peace with one another" (1 Thessalonians 5:13). How can we do that? Jesus speaks about having salt in ourselves and links it with being at peace with one another. What does He mean by that? Salt can only become "unsalty" by being diluted with other things. Jesus is telling us to have undiluted lives, lives that are free of selfishness and self-interest as much as possible. These cause unrest in our hearts and conflict with others. The less "self" we have getting in the way, the less irritant we will be to ourselves or to others. Sometimes as we try to live at peace with others, they are the ones that are the irritant because of their selfishness getting in the way. Being unwilling to forgive one another can be a real "peace breaker." We can't control the actions of others, but we are responsible for ourselves. Remember what Paul says: "If possible, <u>so far as it depends on you</u>, be at peace with all men" (Romans 12:18).

Sometimes forgiveness on our part will be a necessity if peace is ever to be a reality. Jesus says, "You are the salt of the earth" (Matthew 5:13). The ability to create thirst is one thing salt is able to do. Our lives should make others thirst for God. This includes Christians and non-Christians. When we are not at peace with others in the body because of offenses or unforgiveness, we will not be able to draw them closer to God. Even worse, when the world sees Christians unable to get along with one another, our salt (influence w/ world) loses its savor. We get in the way of them having a thirst for God. Paul warns the Jews, "You who boast in the Law, through your breaking the Law, do you dishonor God? For the name of God is blasphemed among the Gentiles because of you" (Romans 2:23-24). If our faith doesn't make enough difference in our lives to make us at peace with each other, it isn't very attractive to those far from God. On the other hand, Jesus says, "By this will all men know that you are My disciples, if you have love for one another" (John 13:35). What is God saying to you about walking in peace with Him or with others?

Food for thought

God wants His church to be a community of peacemakers, especially with one another.

ACTS PRAYING

A - **ADORATION** - Take some time to praise God for who He is, identifying some of His attributes you find particularly meaningful. You may want to express your heart to Him in a journal.

C - **CONFESSION** - Remember, don't go looking for something to confess; that is introspection. Instead ask God to search your heart and to bring to mind anything that needs to be dealt with.

T - **THANKSGIVING** - Thank God for the many blessings of your life, taking a moment to ask God what you need to be thankful for.

S - **SUPPLICATION** - Pray for God to working in your life as you seek to assume your role in helping the body become the kind of community God desires. Bring to Him any requests and needs that are on your heart.

Day 4: The Danger of Being Isolated

"Then it happened in the spring, at the time when kings go out to battle, that David sent Joab and his servants with him and all Israel, and they destroyed the sons of Ammon and besieged Rabbah. But David stayed at Jerusalem. Now when evening came David arose from his bed and walked around on the roof of the king's house, and from the roof he saw a woman bathing; and the woman was very beautiful in appearance. So David sent and inquired about the woman. And one said, "Is this not Bathsheba, the daughter of Eliam, the wife of Uriah the Hittite?" David sent messengers and took her, and when she came to him, he lay with her; and when she had purified herself from her uncleanness, she returned to her house."

– 2 Samuel 11:1-4

In the spring of the year when his armies went to war, David stayed home, alone and isolated, and fell prey to his greatest sin. It is no secret that we are more vulnerable to temptation and attack when we are alone. Even before the fall, God said of Adam, "It is not good for the man to be alone; I will make him a helper suitable for him" (Genesis 2:18). Why do we isolate ourselves as Christians? This is an important question to grapple with as we seek to apply this week's study. Sometimes we isolate to insulate …to protect ourselves. Perhaps the driving motivation is fear, shaped by insecurities and negative experiences from our upbringing. Maybe we go it alone because we are avoiding past pain. It is possible that we isolate ourselves because we are uncomfortable being vulnerable with people who know our junk. Sometimes isolation stems from avoiding conflict and confrontation. Some of us do it to punish others who've hurt us. One reason for isolation and avoiding community is as a consequence of sin – both specific sins and our general sin nature. Sin always creates distance between us and God, and between us and each other. From the very beginning, going all the way back to Genesis 3 and the failure of Adam and Eve in the garden, sin has caused us to hide from each other and from God. Another reason for isolation is simply a choice of our pride and flesh. Perhaps we don't want to be accountable for our actions. Pride whispers the lie that we don't need help…that we can handle things on our own. Has your own sin isolated you?

We all likely remember the story Jesus taught in Luke 15 known as the "parable of the Prodigal Son." The prodigal wanted to enjoy his inheritance without having to wait for it. When it was given by his father, he left his community behind, and with it, the accountability, encouragement, and support he had long taken for granted. When he had squandered away his resources, hard times fell and he found himself alone and unvalued, working in a pig sty with less to eat that the pigs. He only found restoration and redemption when he returned to his father and the community that cared about him. One of the most important realities in a person's life is who you do life with. Perhaps the greatest social epidemic of our time is loneliness. It is a huge issue in modern culture with huge consequences.

Recently I came across an article that first appeared in USA Today in May of 2018. The author related that loneliness and isolation doesn't just make us sad – It can literally make us sick. Drawing on research funded by Cigna, a leading U.S. health insurance provider, the article reported that loneliness actually has the same effect on mortality as smoking fifteen cigarettes a day – even more dangerous than obesity. The article went on to say that "face-to-face conversation is the antidote." Many today spend their spare time at home, alone. They eat alone. Perhaps they watch television or play video games by themselves. Far too many people feel alienated, lonely, and depressed. The hectic pace of life so encroaches that we don't think we have enough time for relationships and for spending time with others in community. I find it ironic that in this day of social media, we are becoming less social than ever. Social media creates an artificial sense of omnipresence – enabling us to virtually connect so many other places that it can have the unintended result of keeping us from truly engaging where we are. Texting, emailing, and social networking through mediums like Facebook or Instagram aren't bad habits in themselves, but real, human interaction cannot be replaced by modern technology. They can help us be aware of what is going on in the lives of others as part of our interaction with them. But if they take the place of face-to-face, heart-to-heart, human interaction, we have traded real community for a façade and something deep in our souls begins to suffer.

THE COMMUNITY GOD WANTS US TO BE

Food for thought

God wants His body to be a community that sees the importance of not isolating from one another.

ACTS PRAYING

A - **ADORATION** - Take some time to praise God for who He is, identifying some of His attributes you find particularly meaningful. You may want to express your heart to Him in a journal.

C - **CONFESSION** - Remember, don't go looking for something to confess; that is introspection. Instead ask God to search your heart and to bring to mind anything that needs to be dealt with.

T - **THANKSGIVING** - Thank God for the many blessings of your life, taking a moment to ask God what you need to be thankful for.

S - **SUPPLICATION** - Pray for God to working in your life as you seek to assume your role in helping the body become the kind of community God desires. Bring to Him any requests and needs that are on your heart.

Day 5: Community Matters

"Two are better than one because they have a good return for their labor. For if either of them falls, the one will lift up his companion. But woe to the one who falls when there is not another to lift him up. Furthermore, if two lie down together they keep warm, but how can one be warm alone? And if one can overpower him who is alone, two can resist him. A cord of three strands is not quickly torn apart."

- Ecclesiastes 4:9-12

King Solomon of the Old Testament is history's wealthiest and wisest king. Because of his great intelligence, he could've thought he didn't need anyone else. Certainly, he was capable of making every decision by himself. With his tremendous wealth, he had the potential to depend on his own resources. If anyone could get away with flying solo, it was Solomon. Instead, he built a team of advisors around himself. He was wise enough to know that he didn't know it all and couldn't do it all. In these few short verses we find some pretty wise advice on why community matters – why we need to do life together as believers. Solomon offers four illustrations from everyday life – working together, stumbling, keeping warm, and being attacked – on why we shouldn't be "Lone Ranger" Christians and should instead learn to live in community with each other.

The "Lone Ranger" is a fictional character who first appeared as an American radio program in the 1930's. The show proved to be a hit and its success spawned a series of books, a long running television show and several movie adaptations. The basic plot involved a Texas Ranger who purportedly was the sole survivor of a group of six Rangers who were ambushed while in pursuit of a band of outlaws. A Native American named Tonto comes across the scene and finds this one Ranger barely alive. He cares for The Lone Ranger until his health is restored and then assists him in his quest for justice in the

North American old west. The masked character is an endearing and enduring American icon, along with his sidekick, Tonto, and trusty horse, "Silver."

While the idea of a "Lone Ranger" has a romantic appeal, he is not a good model for how believers should approach living out their faith. Far too many Christians approach try to "go it alone." They may attend church services and worship in the larger gathering of believers — or they may simply avail themselves of technological ways to experience services. Maybe they listen on the radio or watch live streaming gatherings via the internet. They see the importance of the content of evangelical worship without grasping the community side of Christianity. These "Lone Ranger" Christians live out the bulk of their faith as if it were a solo sport. The irony is that even the original Lone Ranger wasn't alone. He always had is friend Tonto with him.

A great many churches are evaluating themselves these days, trying to figure out why their attendance is shrinking. They may have great programs and lots of activity, but the common concern being voiced quite often is that what's missing is community. This shouldn't be surprising. Real, authentic community is going missing in our culture as a whole. While fifty years ago it was common to build close-knit relationships with our neighbors, in many areas people live in proximity and don't even know each other's names, let alone what is going on in each other's lives. Family units are fractured by relational dysfunctions and job relocation logistics in a highly mobile and transient society. Many people today feel isolated and alone. I believe this presents a great opportunity for reaching people for churches that do well at community, but it isn't happening as broadly as it should. Even in churches with great opportunities for community, not everyone is taking advantage and plugging in. Some believers just don't see the need.

Food for thought

God wants His church to be a community where we don't try to go it alone, but live interconnected with each other.

ACTS PRAYING

A - **ADORATION** - Take some time to praise God for who He is, identifying some of His attributes you find particularly meaningful. You may want to express your heart to Him in a journal.

C - **CONFESSION** - Remember, don't go looking for something to confess; that is introspection. Instead ask God to search your heart and to bring to mind anything that needs to be dealt with.

T - **THANKSGIVING** - Thank God for the many blessings of your life, taking a moment to ask God what you need to be thankful for.

S - **SUPPLICATION** - Pray for God to working in your life as you seek to assume your role in helping the body become the kind of community God desires. Bring to Him any requests and needs that are on your heart.

WEEK SIX
"Forgive One Another"

Day 1: Releasing Our Grievances

"And forgive us our debts, as we also have forgiven our debtors…For if you forgive others for their transgressions, your heavenly Father will also forgive you. But if you do not forgive others, then your Father will not forgive your transgressions."

- Matthew 6:12-15

When we recite the Lord's Prayer, I'm not sure we understand what we are actually praying. Do we really want God to show us the same kind of forgiveness that we show each other? The Greek word translated "forgive" here is *aphiemi* and it paints an interesting picture. It literally means "to release, to let go." What does that have to do with forgiveness? If you will think back to someone you were slow to forgive or perhaps have not forgiven to this day, you will know that when you have chosen not to forgive you have chosen to **hold on to his or her offense**. You were not (or are not) willing to **let it go**. When we forgive someone, we release him or her from the penalty we want to impose (or that we may want God to impose). We release them from the prison of our hateful glares or our cold stares or our ignore-them-at-all-costs actions. God does not want us being prison wardens, keeping others locked up in our penitentiary of unforgiveness. He knows that if we do not forgive, we are the real prisoners, bound by bitterness and anger and hate. Forgiveness is really a matter of faith. Can we trust God to deal with the wrong they may have done us, or do we hold on to vengeance as a right? To the Romans Paul writes, "Never pay back evil for evil to anyone…If possible, so far as it depends on you, be at peace with all men. Never take your own revenge, beloved, but leave room for the wrath of God, for it is written, 'Vengeance is Mine, I will repay,' says the Lord" (Romans 12:17-19). Can we trust God that if someone needs to be punished He will do the right thing in the right way? Or do we fear He will choose grace when we want justice?

God wants us to be "releasers" like Him. He releases us from our sin by His own loving death for that sin. In dying, He paid for that sin fully and now we can know the joy of freedom and of being released to walk with Him in open, honest fellowship. What an incredible gift! He wants us to walk that way with one another also. Romans 15:7 instructs, "Therefore, accept one another, just as Christ also accepted us to the glory of God." God wants His body to be marked by showing grace to one another. That means releasing others, not holding them captive to our opinions, emotions, attitudes, or judgments. The phrase, "forgive us our debts, as we also have forgiven our debtors" is followed by "do not lead us into temptation, but deliver us from evil." One temptation to avoid and evil to be delivered from is unforgiveness, for it leads us to additional sins of pride and self-righteousness. When we stubbornly refuse to forgive, our prayers and enjoyment of God's grace are both hindered. Of all the subjects Christ addresses in His prayer, forgiveness is the only one He isolates for amplification. Verses 14-15 are not saying that believers earn God's forgiveness by forgiving others, for this would run contrary to salvation by grace. However, if we refuse to forgive one another, it keeps us from experiencing the benefits of God's forgiveness. If we rightly understand God's forgiveness of our own sins, then we <u>will</u> have a readiness to forgive others. When we make the **choice** to forgive another, God gives us the empowering **grace** to forgive. Time with one another is so much better when we are walking in grace. So forgive one another and experience that grace.

Food for thought

God wants His body to be a community that is characterized by showing the grace of forgiveness to one another.

ACTS PRAYING

A - **ADORATION** - Take some time to praise God for who He is, identifying some of His attributes you find particularly meaningful. You may want to express your heart to Him in a journal.

C - **CONFESSION** - Remember, don't go looking for something to confess; that is introspection. Instead ask God to search your heart and to bring to mind anything that needs to be dealt with.

T - **THANKSGIVING** - Thank God for the many blessings of your life, taking a moment to ask God what you need to be thankful for.

S - **SUPPLICATION** - Pray for God to working in your life as you seek to assume your role in helping the body become the kind of community God desires. Bring to Him any requests and needs that are on your heart.

Day 2: Time To Change Clothes

"Let all bitterness and wrath and anger and clamor and slander be put away from you, along with all malice. And be kind to one another, tender-hearted, **forgiving each other**, just as God in Christ also has forgiven you."

- Ephesians 4:31-32

In a fallen world populated by fallen people, offenses are inevitable. When we hold on to our grievances against others instead of forgiving, we grow in our bitterness (hurt) and wrath (flaring up) and anger (flaring out at them) and clamor (making noise) and slander (cutting them down). With that we also grow in our malice—we want to hurt them or see them hurt to pay for what they did to us. Ours is a sin-stained world, but the church need not be a sin-stained community. Indeed, it must not be such a place. Colossians 3:13 reiterates this value, calling us to "Bear with each other and **forgive** whatever grievances you may have against one another. **Forgive** as the Lord forgave you." God wants His church to be a community where we are kind to one another, forgiving each other as we have been forgiven. Ephesians 4:25 even reminds us of why it is so important how we treat each other: "for we are members of one another." But, that kind of community won't be a reality until we first "put away" these attributes of ugliness that Paul lists.

How do we "put away" the actions and attitudes mentioned in verse 31? The answer lies in the context of Ephesians 4. These actions and attitudes are part of the "old self." In Ephesians 4:22-24 Paul says we are to "lay aside the old self, which is being corrupted in accordance with the lusts of deceit…be renewed in the spirit of [our] mind, and put on the new self which in the likeness of God has been created in righteousness and holiness of the truth." Here in Ephesians 4 the apostle Paul speaks metaphorically of our spiritual state as clothing or as a garment. Before salvation all we possessed were the filthy rags of sin, and thus had no choice but to wear them. At salvation we were fitted with holy and righteous garments ("clothed with Christ") called the "new self" (literally "new person"). Yet in order for Christ to be ours in experience, we must take off the old garment and put on the new. He exhorts us to pull it off the hanger each morning and make it our chosen attire. What is this new garment? It is Jesus.

The Prophet Zechariah cautions, "do not devise evil in your hearts against one another" (Zech. 7:10). Is there anyone for whom you "devise evil" in your heart? In order to be kind and forgiving we must "lay aside" the rags of the old person as an act of the will through confession and repentance. This concept is not simply referring to salvation since this is written to believers. We must also "put on" the new garment which is Christ by yielding that area to Christ's control and depending on Him. Part of a long-range plan for victory must also be cultivating a renewed mind – allowing God's Word to convict us of sinful attitudes and actions and teach us to view each area of our lives from His perspective. The application he desires is obvious, but the choice is ours. We have new clothes – beautiful, spotless garments. Yet, amazingly, we can and sometimes do still wear the filthy rags of our old, fallen existence – the rags of bitterness, wrath, anger, malice, and unforgiveness. Our selection of garments is a choice. What Paul calls us to is a lifestyle of consistently dressing in the new garments of Christ – clothing ourselves in righteousness and holiness. It takes kindness and a tender heart to forgive. If we are wearing the new garments, we <u>will</u> be kind to one another, and we will be able to forgive each other the way Christ forgives. What are you going to wear today?

Food for thought

God wants His church to be a community where we are kind to one another, forgiving one another as we have been forgiven.

ACTS PRAYING

A - **ADORATION** - Take some time to praise God for who He is, identifying some of His attributes you find particularly meaningful. You may want to express your heart to Him in a journal.

C - **CONFESSION** - Remember, don't go looking for something to confess; that is introspection. Instead ask God to search your heart and to bring to mind anything that needs to be dealt with.

T - **THANKSGIVING** - Thank God for the many blessings of your life, taking a moment to ask God what you need to be thankful for.

S - **SUPPLICATION** - Pray for God to working in your life as you seek to assume your role in helping the body become the kind of community God desires. Bring to Him any requests and needs that are on your heart.

Day 3: The Consequences of Not Forgiving One Another

"Therefore let us not judge one another anymore, but rather determine this-- not to put an obstacle or a stumbling block in a brother's way."

- Romans 14:13

Not only do the Scriptures give us clear advice on our responsibilities to one another, they also instructs us as to what should not be a part of our relationships with each other. Just as "knots" in a board hinder the carpenter in his work, these "nots" in relationships get in the way and hinder our fellowship. God desires that we clean these "nots" out of our relationships. One act to avoid is judging one another. In essence what Paul is saying is "instead of worrying about what someone else is doing, you ought to be worrying about your own behavior and how to not give cause for others to judge you!" Paul has much to say about what should not be part of our relationships with one another. In 1 Thessalonians 5:15 he writes, "See that no one repays another with evil for evil, but always seek after that which is good for one another and for all people." If someone does us wrong and we do wrong back to them, it doesn't make them stop and say, "I shouldn't have done that to them." It just makes them want to retaliate all the more and the cycle keeps repeating itself. In Galatians 5:15 he warns, "But if you bite and devour one another, take care that you are not consumed by one another." When we seek what is best instead of repaying evil with evil, we break the cycle. The added phrase "…and for all people" gives an important clarification. If we only seek the best of the offending person in could be mere appeasement. There are times when we need to confront evil for the sake of preventing it from hurting others. Even then, we cannot address evil with evil. If we have not first forgiven the offender, we give place in our hearts for evil.

Paul adds other "nots" to our One Another list in his letter to the churches of Galatia. In Galatians 5:26 we read, "Let us not become boastful, challenging one another, envying one another." To be boastful is the attitude of thinking more highly of ourselves which says without merit, "I'm the right one." To challenge one another communicates we know with certainty "You are the wrong one." The word literally means "to call before" and has the idea of making someone answer to you. To envy is the attitude of coveting another's success and saying, "You are right, but I wish it was me instead." All of these wrongs Paul places in contrast to walking "by the Spirit" (Galatians 5:25). To the Colossians Paul admonishes, "…put them all aside: anger, wrath, malice, slander, and abusive speech from your mouth. Do not lie to one another, since you laid aside the old self with its evil practices" (Colossians 3:9). All of these sinful attitudes and actions can grow in a heart that refuses to forgive. Think about how Paul expresses this. They <u>already</u> laid aside the old self with its evil practices at salvation. The fact that Paul is telling them to put aside these evil practices shows that, although we are freed from bondage to our old nature, we can still go there through wrong choices. One shortcut to this wrong destination is unforgiveness. The very fact that we are instructed not to do these things indicates that within the power of God's Spirit directing our lives, we have the ability to lay these things aside. It becomes an issue of the will – "Am I willing to surrender my rights and desires to God's will for my relationships?" As we choose to act in accordance with God's revealed will (Scripture) we can trust that blessing will follow. If we walk after the flesh, we hurt one another, <u>and</u> we fail to minister to one another as we should.

Food for thought

God wants His body to be a community that always seeks after that which is good for one another.

ACTS PRAYING

A - **ADORATION** - Take some time to praise God for who He is, identifying some of His attributes you find particularly meaningful. You may want to express your heart to Him in a journal.

C - **CONFESSION** - Remember, don't go looking for something to confess; that is introspection. Instead ask God to search your heart and to bring to mind anything that needs to be dealt with.

T - **THANKSGIVING** - Thank God for the many blessings of your life, taking a moment to ask God what you need to be thankful for.

S - **SUPPLICATION** - Pray for God to working in your life as you seek to assume your role in helping the body become the kind of community God desires. Bring to Him any requests and needs that are on your heart.

Day 4: Judged for Judging

"Do not complain, brethren, against one another, that you yourselves may not be judged; behold, the Judge is standing right at the door."

- James 5:9

When the Pharisees confront Jesus with a woman caught in adultery, they demand He pass judgment on her. Instead of answering, Jesus draws in the dirt with His finger. The Bible does not tell us what He writes on the ground, but some suggest that He is writing out the Ten Commandments. After being pressed for an answer, He replies, "He who is without sin among you, let him be the first to throw a stone at her" (John 8:7). One by one the Pharisees quietly walk away. We do not realize it, but every time we pass judgment on a fellow Christian, we are also passing judgment on ourselves. We may not have committed the specific crime of the one we are complaining against, but by judging another we are asking to operate on the basis of justice. If we are going to demand justice of another, we must accept the same accountability ourselves. Do we really want justice when it is applied to our actions, or do we want mercy?

One day Peter comes to Jesus and asks, "Lord, how often shall my brother sin against me and I forgive him? Up to seven times?" (Matthew 18:21). The Pharisees taught that you only have to forgive someone three times, so Peter probably thinks he is being generous. In effect, the teaching of the day is that forgiveness is more like probation – it only lasts if the offender keeps his nose clean. Peter is not prepared for Jesus' answer: "I do not say to you, up to seven times, but up to seventy times seven" (Matthew 18:22). The Lord then offers a parable so that Peter can understand true forgiveness. He tells the story of a king who is owed a great sum of money – ten thousand talents. That represents about a hundred and fifty years wages for a laborer, so there is no way this common man will be able to pay the debt. The king prepares to sell the man and his family as slaves, but when he falls to the ground and begs for mercy, the king feels compassion for him and forgives his debt. You would think someone who has just experienced mercy to such a great degree would be flooded with mercy for others, but that is not human nature. This man finds a friend who owes him a hundred denarii – a trifling sum in comparison – and when he can't pay, the man has him thrown in jail. Word reaches the king, who summons him and says, "You wicked slave, I forgave you all that debt because you pleaded with me. 'Should you not also have had mercy on your fellow slave, in the same way that I had mercy on you?' " (Matthew 18:32-33). The angry master hands him over to the torturers until his debt is paid.

We probably don't realize it, but when we demand justice from others and grumble and complain when we don't get it, we are asking to operate by a different standard than the mercy God has shown to us. We know we stand before God always and only by His grace and mercy, yet in our relationships with each other we tend to expect and demand justice. James admonishes us to lay down our complaints against our brother or sister. If we demand perfect justice for them, we are inviting our own lives to be held to the same standard. I don't think that is really what we want. Earlier in his epistle, James writes, "So speak and so act as those who are to be judged by the law of liberty. For judgment will be merciless to one who has shown no mercy; mercy triumphs over justice" (James 2:12-13). A right relationship with God hinges on His forgiving our sins, but the outflow of that should be forgiving our brother or sister.

Food for thought

God wants His body to be a community that shows one another the same grace He shows us, and leaves judgment to Him.

ACTS PRAYING

A - **ADORATION** - Take some time to praise God for who He is, identifying some of His attributes you find particularly meaningful. You may want to express your heart to Him in a journal.

C - **CONFESSION** - Remember, don't go looking for something to confess; that is introspection. Instead ask God to search your heart and to bring to mind anything that needs to be dealt with.

T - **THANKSGIVING** - Thank God for the many blessings of your life, taking a moment to ask God what you need to be thankful for.

S - **SUPPLICATION** - Pray for God to working in your life as you seek to assume your role in helping the body become the kind of community God desires. Bring to Him any requests and needs that are on your heart.

Day 5: Pursuing Peace

"So then let us pursue the things which make for peace and the building up of one another."

– Romans 14:19

What does it mean to be a "peacemaker"? Paul clearly calls us to peace as a pursuit. Yet he does not instruct us to pursue peace as an end in itself. Rather, we are to pursue the "things which make for peace" with one another. We cannot control whether there will be peace, but we can pursue peacemaking. To fully appreciate Paul's point, we need to understand the context. He is discussing the need for each believer to have convictions, not mere opinions. He charges us to use these convictions to guide our own behavior, not to judge another. What has this to do with forgiving one another? Think about the two sides of the issues Paul addresses in Romans 14. He gives examples of one who eats meat and another who thinks it wrong. He references the person who judges one day of the week (presumably the Sabbath) as above the others, and another who treats all days the same. The destination he challenges them toward is to study the matter fully, for "…each person must be fully convinced in his own mind" (Romans 14:5). The problem is we tend to make up our minds without studying the matter fully. Paul starts the chapter saying, "Now accept the one who is weak in faith, but not for the purpose of passing judgment on his opinions" (Romans 14:1). In other words, forgive him or her for not having fully developed convictions. If we don't forgive their imperfections, we will find ourselves "passing judgment" on their opinions. Since "each person must be fully convinced," we must allow for the possibility that we don't have it all figured out either.

But what about when we really are right? First of all, it probably isn't as many times as we think. But equally important, even if we are right, there is more at stake than our rights. In Romans 14:7 Paul reminds, "For not one of us lives for himself…". Self should not be the only or even the main consideration. If we are right and the other is wrong and we demand our way, we say by action that the other person doesn't matter. Paul points out, "if because of food your brother is hurt, you are not walking according to love. Do not destroy with your food him for whom Christ died" (Romans 14:15). If we do that, instead of pursuing peace we are pursuing conflict and position ourselves to be the one in need of forgiveness. That's not what God wants the body to be like. God wants His church to be a community where we walk with one another according to love. We need to be working for "the building up of one another." To pursue peace means that even if we are right, we are willing to not demand our rights. Who knows? Perhaps by our deference, we can earn the right to be heard and bring others to a more mature position. That is a worthy pursuit.

To be a "peacemaker" means not only that one lives peaceably but also that he or she is an agent of peace in the lives of others. In the Beatitudes, Jesus pronounces, "Blessed are the peacemakers, for they shall be called the sons of God" (Matthew 5:9). The text does not tell us such a one _is_ a child of God, though certainly that seems to be assumed. The text emphasizes that a peacemaker not only is a child of God, but through making peace others begin to recognize him or her as such. They see in the child the character of the Father. God is pleased when we pursue peace with one another, and let's face it – the body is a more enjoyable place to be when we get along with one another.

Food for thought

God wants His church to be a community where we walk with one another according to love and pursue peace.

ACTS PRAYING

A - **ADORATION** - Take some time to praise God for who He is, identifying some of His attributes you find particularly meaningful. You may want to express your heart to Him in a journal.

C - **CONFESSION** - Remember, don't go looking for something to confess; that is introspection. Instead ask God to search your heart and to bring to mind anything that needs to be dealt with.

T - **THANKSGIVING** - Thank God for the many blessings of your life, taking a moment to ask God what you need to be thankful for.

S - **SUPPLICATION** - Pray for God to working in your life as you seek to assume your role in helping the body become the kind of community God desires. Bring to Him any requests and needs that are on your heart.

WEEK SEVEN
"Minister to One Another"

Day 1: Stewardship of Serving

"As each one has received a special gift, employ it in serving one another as good stewards of the manifold grace of God. Whoever speaks, is to do so as one who is speaking the utterances of God; whoever serves is to do so as one who is serving by the strength which God supplies; so that in all things God may be glorified through Jesus Christ, to whom belongs the glory and dominion forever and ever. Amen."

- 1 Peter 4:10-11

Peter begins these verses with an assumption – "each one has received a special gift." He is speaking, of course, of what the Bible calls spiritual gifts. In Ephesians 4:8 Paul quotes the Old Testament prophecy, "When He ascended on high, He led captive a host of captives, and He gave gifts to men" (Psalm 68:18), and interprets it as having been fulfilled by Christ giving us spiritual gifts. Everyone has at least one. That means we all have some kind of ministry to contribute. Since none of us possesses all the gifts, it is guaranteed that we will need what others have to contribute. God has assured that His body will be a community of interdependence – we need each other. But notice what Peter says we are to do with our giftedness: "employ it in serving one another as good stewards of the manifold grace of God." For God's intent to be realized, our gift must be employed, or put to work. Peter clarifies that more than just a gift, it is a stewardship – we will answer to God for what we did with what He gave us. When Christ ascended, having saved us and forgiven our sins, He freed us from bondage to sin. He did not free us to selfishly live however we wanted, though. Galatians 5:13 teaches, "For you were called to freedom, brethren; only do not turn your freedom into an opportunity for the flesh, but through love serve one another."

True fellowship is not self-serving, it focuses on meeting the needs of others. When I choose to meet someone else's needs instead of striving to meet my own, it is an act of faith. I am trusting God, and not self-effort, to meet the needs of my heart. I love the one I serve. Either I love self and serving self, or I love the Father and serving Him and those who are His. God wants His body to be a community where we all "serve one another" through love. An important way we serve each other is through our gifts. In 1 Peter, the emphasis is on the two overall categories of giftedness: speaking and serving. In a practical sense, all of us minister by speaking (what we say) and serving (what we do). God wants both of these to be done the right manner. Whenever we speak, we should speak "the utterances of God" – we should say what God would say in that situation.

Whenever we serve, we should do so "by the strength that God supplies" – we should do it in His strength, not in our own. When we say what God wants said and we serve in God's strength, the resulting fruit brings glory to God, not to us. This is God's perfect plan. We were created to glorify our Maker, not ourselves. He is the one "to whom belongs the glory and dominion forever and ever."

Food for thought

God wants His body to be a community where through love, we all "serve one another."

ACTS PRAYING

A - **ADORATION** - Take some time to praise God for who He is, identifying some of His attributes you find particularly meaningful.

C - **CONFESSION** - Remember, don't go looking for something to confess; that is introspection. Instead ask God to search your heart and to bring to mind anything that needs to be dealt with.

T - **THANKSGIVING** - Thank God for the many blessings of your life, taking a moment to ask God what you need to be thankful for.

S - **SUPPLICATION** - Pray for God's working in your life as you seek to assume your role in helping the body become the community God desires. Bring to Him any requests and needs that are on your heart.

Day 2: Be Hospitable to One Another

"Above all, keep fervent in your love for one another, because love covers a multitude of sins. Be hospitable to one another without complaint."

- 1 Peter 4:8-9

Peter admonishes us to "keep fervent in your love for one another," and immediately follows this admonition with another: "Be hospitable to one another." One naturally flows to the other. What comes to mind when you hear the word "hospitality"? Most men think of it as "women's work," but that is not a Biblical perspective. In fact, hospitality is one of the Scriptural requirements for church leadership. In the two main passages on the qualifications of an elder, the same Greek word for "hospitable" here (*philoxenos*) is used.[5] It literally means "friend (*philos*) to strangers (*xenos*)." It refers to showing kindness and hospitality to someone who is a guest in one's house or family. In Peter's day there wasn't a Holiday Inn Express in every town or a Motel 6 leaving the light on for you. Instead, it was a priority in Jewish culture for all to have the hospitality to open up their homes to travelers. The writer of Hebrews admonished, "Let love of the brethren continue. Do not neglect to show hospitality to strangers, for by this some have entertained angels without knowing it" (Hebrews 13:2). Peter exhorted the believers to show hospitality with a good attitude; without grumbling or complaining. Because they were opening up their homes and giving to the needs of others, there could be the temptation to murmur or complain about the ways some acted. Perhaps this "stranger" would expect more than one would think is right or they may seem to take advantage of the situation or of the hospitality. Peter told us to watch out for a begrudging attitude.

---

[5] See 1 Timothy 3:2 and Titus 1:8

Speaking of giving in 2 Corinthians 8:8, Paul reminds us that actions are a way we prove "the sincerity of [our] love." In 2 Corinthians 9:7 he instructs that our giving should be planned and intentional. He says, "Each one must do just as he as purposed in his heart," but Paul doesn't stop there. It's also about our attitude. Paul finishes saying, "not grudgingly or under compulsion, for God loves a cheerful giver." There really are three steps here. First, we must "purpose in our heart." We must decide to be a giver, whether by time or talents or treasure. The truly hospitable person is so because of character and choice, not circumstances. But there is a second aspect to Paul's ambition for us. Good intentions aren't enough. We must follow through and "do" what we purpose. But even that is not enough. God wants us to purpose (be intentional), to do (take action), AND to do what we have purposed with a good attitude. Paul uses the adjective "cheerful" to describe what kind of giver we are to be. The Greek word (*hilaros*) is the source of our English term "hilarious", but don't let that mislead you. The Greek term doesn't carry the idea of frivolity and being overcome with laughter associated with our English word. *Hilaros* denotes a happy, joyous or cheerful state of mind.

When we talk about showing hospitality we are not talking about "entertaining." That can be expensive and is sometimes done just to impress others. Entertaining isn't necessarily from the heart. When we have an open heart to others, then we are willing to help where we can which includes opening our home. It is more work, but it is worth it. We see that we are investing in relationships that matter. We are building into the lives of others, whether for a youth group or college kids, a care group or several couples. What matters is using the opportunity to show love to others. That is the heart of Romans 12:10 and 13: "Be devoted to one another in brotherly love; give preference to one another in honor; …contributing to the needs of the saints, practicing hospitality." Let's close with the apostle John adding a final thought. "But whoever has the world's goods, and beholds his brother in need and closes his heart against him, how does the love of God abide in him? Little children, let us not love with word or with tongue, but in deed and truth" (1 John 3:17-18).

Food for thought

God wants His body to be a community characterized by heart-felt hospitality.

ACTS PRAYING

<u>**A**</u> - <u>**ADORATION**</u> - Take some time to praise God for who He is, identifying some of His attributes you find particularly meaningful.

<u>**C**</u> - <u>**CONFESSION**</u> - Remember, don't go looking for something to confess; that is introspection. Instead ask God to search your heart and to bring to mind anything that needs to be dealt with.

<u>**T**</u> - <u>**THANKSGIVING**</u> - Thank God for the many blessings of your life, taking a moment to ask God what you need to be thankful for.

<u>**S**</u> - <u>**SUPPLICATION**</u> - Pray for God's working in your life as you seek to assume your role in helping the body become the community God desires. Bring to Him any requests and needs that are on your heart.

Day 3: Using Our Mouth for Ministry

"Do not speak against one another, brethren. He who speaks against a brother, or judges his brother, speaks against the law, and judges the law; but if you judge the law, you are not a doer of the law, but a judge of it. There is only one Lawgiver and Judge, the One who is able to save and to destroy; but who are you who judge your neighbor?"

- James 4:11-12

Not all Scriptural "One Anothers" are positive admonitions. Some tell us how <u>not</u> to treat each other. James 3 makes it clear that the tongue is a powerful tool both for good and for evil. What does God desire in His family? "Do not speak against one another" is a command (an imperative in the Greek), not a suggestion. The kind of "speaking against" referenced by James is judging our brother or sister (fellow Christian). Human pride wants to draw our own worth by comparing ourselves to those around us. When we judge, we always do so in such a way that the sin of the other is magnified and ours is belittled. This is what the Pharisee was doing in Luke 18:9-14 (read this if you have time). He boasted that he was not like other men, yet our call is to be like God. One reason God does not allow us to judge is because we are unable to do it fairly. "Rare is the man who can weigh the faults of another without putting his finger on the scales." In 1 Corinthians 4:5 Paul shows us how God judges: He will "bring to light the things hidden in darkness and disclose the motives of men's hearts." We are unfit to judge because there is always something hidden we do not see, and we are unable to see the heart motive of another.

James makes clear, "There is only one Lawgiver and Judge." His point here is that only the one who gave the Law has a right to hold people accountable to it. The good news here is that the Lawgiver is not only able to punish, but also to save or rescue from punishment. When we judge, we can destroy but we can never save. "Who are you who judge your neighbor?" Paul asks a similar question in Romans 14:4, "Who are you to judge the servant of another? To his own master he stands or falls; and stand he will, for the Lord is able to make him stand." We can be used of the Lord in that process, but not if our tongues are busy tearing down. Paul concludes in Romans 14:19, "So then let us pursue the things which make for peace and the building up of one another." We are to chase after peacemaking and building up one another. Our mouths were made for ministry, not maligning. So, how do we use our mouths rightly, not wrongly? Peter exhorts, "…be harmonious, sympathetic, brotherly, kindhearted, and humble in spirit; not returning evil for evil, or insult for insult, but giving a blessing instead; for you were called for the very purpose that you might inherit a blessing" (1 Peter 3:8-9). There are many practical words of advice in this package. We should seek harmony. We should have humility. We should avoid retaliating. We should give a blessing instead. It is important however, to realize that if the wrong things are coming off our tongues toward one another, the solution is not to "bite our tongues" and stop saying those things. James 3:8 teaches us that "no one can tame the tongue." The reason for this is bound in what Jesus says in Matthew 12:34 – "the mouth speaks out of that which fills the heart." To change our speech, we must give our hearts over to the Lord's control. If we do, He will bless others through us.

Food for thought

God wants His body to be a community where we use our words to build each other up, not tear each other down.

ACTS PRAYING

A - **ADORATION** - Take some time to praise God for who He is, identifying some of His attributes you find particularly meaningful.

C - **CONFESSION** - Remember, don't go looking for something to confess; that is introspection. Instead ask God to search your heart and to bring to mind anything that needs to be dealt with.

T - **THANKSGIVING** - Thank God for the many blessings of your life, taking a moment to ask God what you need to be thankful for.

S - **SUPPLICATION** - Pray for God's working in your life as you seek to assume your role in helping the body become the community God desires. Bring to Him any requests and needs that are on your heart.

Day 4: Ministering Truth in Love

"And concerning you, my brethren, I myself also am convinced that you yourselves are full of goodness, filled with all knowledge, and able also to admonish one another."

- Romans 15:14

While it is certainly a true statement that our tongues were meant for ministry, not maligning, this doesn't mean we only tell people words they like to hear. We are not to puff each other up with insincere flattery, nor are we to withhold truth that is needed just because it isn't wanted. In order for our tongues to produce ministry, they must speak the truth. Teaching about the body of Christ in Ephesians 4:15, Paul identifies that we are to be "speaking the truth in love" to each other. Notice, we are to speak, not remain silent. We are to speak truth, not flattery or opinion. And we are to do so in love. When we do this, we each "grow up in all aspects into Him who is the Head, even Christ." To use our mouths for ministry, we must be willing to say hard things to each other. In Proverbs 27:5-6 Solomon advised, "Better is open rebuke than love that is concealed. Faithful are the wounds of a friend, But deceitful are the kisses of an enemy." Solomon is saying that to speak, even if the words are hard, is better than to conceal our love for one another with silence. Sometimes the most loving speech is open rebuke. When we do not say what needs to be said, or when we speak insincere words to another we are being their enemy, rather than their friend. Jesus said, "Greater love has no one than this, that one lay down his life for his friends" (John 15:13). We need to be willing to lay ourselves down and speak up. Paul continues in Ephesians 4:25, "...laying aside falsehood, speak truth, each one of you, with his neighbor, for we are members of one another."

If I have food stuck between my teeth or my clothing is somehow out of sorts, I want someone to point it out. They are not being a friend to me if they see a problem and say nothing. Paul says he is convinced we are "able to admonish one another." The word "admonish" means to warn or to exhort. The Greek word literally means "to place before the mind." When we admonish one another, we are not responsible for what the other does with what we say. We can only put it before their minds and leave the response to them and to the work of God's Spirit. But if we remain silent, we may be working against their growth instead of for it. There is an important point to catch in Paul's words here. He is convinced the Romans are able to admonish each other because he is convinced they are "full of goodness" and they are "filled with all knowledge." These are two important prerequisites to admonishing one another. First, we must be full of goodness. Before we speak we must make sure our heart is right. Jesus instructed, "first take the log out of your own eye, and then you will see clearly to take the speck out of your brother's eye" (Matthew 7:5). Second, to admonish rightly we must be filled with _all_ knowledge. This isn't saying we have to know everything about everything. It is saying we need to know the whole story before we speak. Proverbs 12:18 says, "There is one who speaks rashly like the thrusts of a sword." When we speak without thinking we can do a lot of damage. Proverbs 20:25 says, "It is a trap for a man to say rashly, 'It is holy!', and after the vows to make inquiry." Proverbs 18:17 says, "The first to plead his case seems right, until another comes and examines him." Make sure you have heard both sides of the story before you try and admonish your brother.

Food for thought

God wants His church to be a community that speaks the truth in love

ACTS PRAYING

A - **ADORATION** - Take some time to praise God for who He is, identifying some of His attributes you find particularly meaningful.

C - **CONFESSION** - Remember, don't go looking for something to confess; that is introspection. Instead ask God to search your heart and to bring to mind anything that needs to be dealt with.

T - **THANKSGIVING** - Thank God for the many blessings of your life, taking a moment to ask God what you need to be thankful for.

S - **SUPPLICATION** - Pray for God's working in your life as you seek to assume your role in helping the body become the community God desires. Bring to Him any requests and needs that are on your heart.

THE COMMUNITY GOD WANTS US TO BE

Day 5: Being The Answer to Our Prayers

"While they were ministering to the Lord and fasting, the Holy Spirit said, 'Set apart for Me Barnabas and Saul for the work to which I have called them.' "

– Acts 13:2

It is worth noticing that the great thrust of world missions, the first missionary journey of Paul and Barnabas, was born in a season of prayer, not a planning meeting. The leaders were worshipping and fasting. The Greek word translated "ministering" here is *leitourgeo* from which we get our English term "liturgy." It is in the present tense indicating ongoing action. The emphasis seems to be that they were in a season of worship and seeking the Lord as the ministry continued. We don't know the catalyst for their fast, but it was during it that God chose to speak. As we pray for one another, our conversation is not supposed to be one-sided. God wants us to listen to Him, not just read to Him a list of things we want. God's message was clear and unequivocal – He wanted to reassign two of the key leaders in the church. The most obvious reason for the direction of travel Barnabas and Saul chose is the fact that they were "sent out by the Holy Spirit." We trust that not only was the task divinely initiated, but the process as well. We know that Barnabas was originally from Cyprus (Acts 4:36) and would have been familiar with the culture and area. Seleucia was the seaport of Antioch and was the logical route to Cyprus. Think about the implications of this. Antioch was the first primarily Gentile church. We learn in Acts 11:20 that this church was planted by Christians originally from Cyprus. Obviously they would be burdened for their fellow Gentiles to come to know the life-changing message of the gospel. Being from Cyprus, no doubt Barnabas was burdened to pray for his native land. It is logical to assume that they were praying for God to save their countrymen. In the midst of their prayers, God calls them to take part in answering them.

One of the reasons God wants His church to be a community that prays for one another is that through prayer our hearts are drawn toward God's will for the object of our prayers. As we are involved in ministering to them by praying for them, we are most open to God inviting us to minister to them in other ways. Corrie ten Boom's faith was molded in the Nazi concentration camps of World War II. She offers this advice on praying for one another: "We never know how God will answer our prayers, but we can expect that He will get us involved in His plan for the answer. If we are true intercessors, we must be ready to take part in God's work on behalf of the people for whom we pray." As we pray for one another, we must be willing to participate in the answer to those prayers. If we are praying for a need that we have the ability to meet, we need to stop praying and start acting in faith that God will use us to be the answer. If we are willing to pray, but not willing to act, have we not failed to "love one another, just as He commanded us" (1 John 3:23)? We are like the Christians whose faith James condemns in James 2:15-17. He admonishes, "If a brother or sister is without clothing and in need of daily food, and one of you says to them, "Go in peace, be warmed and be filled," and yet you do not give them what is necessary for their body, what use is that? Even so faith, if it has no works, is dead, being by itself." True prayer is an expression of faith, but it cannot be the only way we are willing to show our faith.

Food for thought

God not only wants His church to be a community that prays for one another, He wants us to be open to Him inviting us to minister to them in other ways.

ACTS PRAYING

A - **ADORATION** - Take some time to praise God for who He is, identifying some of His attributes you find particularly meaningful.

C - **CONFESSION** - Remember, don't go looking for something to confess; that is introspection. Instead ask God to search your heart and to bring to mind anything that needs to be dealt with.

T - **THANKSGIVING** - Thank God for the many blessings of your life, taking a moment to ask God what you need to be thankful for.

S - **SUPPLICATION** - Pray for God's working in your life as you seek to assume your role in helping the body become the community God desires. Bring to Him any requests and needs that are on your heart.

WEEK EIGHT
"Love One Another"

Day 1: A New Commandment

"A new commandment I give to you, that you love one another, even as I have loved you, that you also love one another."

- John 13:34

We live in a world of commandments – rules of what we can and cannot do. At a glance, faith may seem to be maintaining a set of rules. After all, didn't God give Moses a top ten list during his forty days on Mount Sinai? In fact, those Ten Commandments were written in stone and carried with Israel wherever they went. Rabbis and theologians continued to refine and redefine the rules throughout the years. What began as ten commands has been expanded into a massive rule book with 613 commands by the time of Jesus' ministry. Faith had become so complicated and confusing that only the professionals could live it. God's guidance for life had become a weighty burden. If this were the way faith was supposed to be lived, one would expect Jesus to applaud it. Instead of complimenting the Pharisees, however, Jesus condemned them as hypocrites. In Matthew 15:7-9 Jesus called their faith "vain worship" because they had turned their own ideas into doctrine. They had become so adept at keeping rules that they were not aware that they had distanced themselves from God. They lost the point that the ultimate objective of every commandment was relationship. The reason we repent of idolatry and Sabbath breaking and taking the Lord's name in vain is for the sake of relationship with God. The reason we repent of stealing and adultery and murder is for the sake of relationship with our fellow man.

One day a lawyer posed a question to Jesus – not a courtroom lawyer like we think of today, but an expert in Mosaic law. He was a legalist

– a "theological nit-picker." Most likely he had already decided which commandment was the greatest and wanted to see if Jesus agreed with him. Christ's answer had to be unexpected. Quoting from Deuteronomy 6:5, Jesus replied, "You shall love the Lord your God with all your heart, and with all your soul, and with all your mind" (Matthew 22:37). Not only did He give an authoritative response, calling it "the greatest and foremost commandment," He also answered the unasked question of which is number two on the list. Referencing Leviticus 19:18, He added, "…You shall love your neighbor as yourself" (Matthew 22:39). Christ made it clear that every other Biblical directive was given to enable us to live out these two relationship mandates. This value is easily seen in the Ten Commandments, as the first four directly deal with our relationship with God and the remaining six deal with our relationships with other people.

We are commanded to love one another with the same kind of committed, unconditional love that God shows us. At the beginning of the "Upper Room Discourse" Jesus uttered this "New Commandment." Before the night was over, He repeated it twice more: "This is My commandment, that you love one another, just as I have loved you" (John 15:12). "This I command you, that you love one another" (John 15:17). I think He wanted to make sure they got the point. It is significant and noteworthy that this desire appears in the last words Jesus prayed before He was arrested in Gethsemane: "…that the love with which You the Father loved Me may be in them, and I in them" (John 17:26). Jesus prays that all who believe would love one another.

Food for thought

How do you think the followers of Christ are doing at loving one another as Christ loved?

ACTS PRAYING

A - **ADORATION** - Take some time to praise God for who He is, identifying some of His attributes you find particularly meaningful. You may want to express your heart to Him in a journal.

C - **CONFESSION** - Remember, don't go looking for something to confess; that is introspection. Instead ask God to search your heart and to bring to mind anything that needs to be dealt with.

T - **THANKSGIVING** - Thank God for the many blessings of your life, taking a moment to ask God what you need to be thankful for.

S - **SUPPLICATION** - Pray for God to working in your life as you seek to assume your role in helping the body become the kind of community God desires. Bring to Him any requests and needs that are on your heart.

Day 2: Love, The Final Apologetic

"By this all men will know that you are My disciples, if you have love for one another"

- John 13:35

Think about the implications of that statement. It will be obvious to everyone that we follow Christ…not by showing love to Him, but if we "have love for one another." The great Christian philosopher Francis Schaeffer called love "the final apologetic" – the ultimate proof of our faith. The word "love" is used in a thousand different ways. We love apple pie, baseball, tennis, mom, and God. We use one word—love—to describe how we feel toward something or someone, but love is much more than that one word and it is certainly more than a feeling that you feel when you feel that way. What does it mean to love one another? We know that this is important to Jesus because He gave this as the new commandment—not new because it had never been commanded before, because Leviticus talks about loving one's neighbor. This new command would be fulfilled with a new power—His Spirit within each heart. We know this command is important to the Father because His children would be "taught by God to love one another" (1 Thess. 4:9). What does it mean then?

Loving one another will mean being real, giving unselfishly, going the extra mile with someone or for someone. It will mean relying on the power of the Spirit – not the pulse of our feelings. It is a choice—sometimes it feels good, sometimes it doesn't. Sometimes it's tough and takes a lot of energy, but we go ahead because it's the right thing to do. Liza was suffering from a rare and serious disease. Her only chance of recovery appeared to be a blood transfusion from her five-year-old brother, who miraculously survived the same disease and had developed the antibodies needed to combat the illness. The doctor explained the situation to her little brother, and asked the boy if he would be willing to give his blood for his sister. He hesitated for a moment and said, "Yes, I'll do it if it will save Liza." As the transfusion progressed, he lay in bed next to his sister and smiled, seeing the color return to her cheeks. Then his face grew pale and his smile faded. He looked up at the doctor and asked with a trembling voice, "Will I start to die right away?" Being young, the boy had misunderstood the doctor. He thought he was going to have to give her all his blood.[6] The little boy had been willing to give his life for his sister's need. That kind of love that puts others before self is what it means to love one another as Christ loved us. That is sincere love. That is fervent love.

---

[6] Canfield, Jack and Mark Victor Hansen. *Chicken Soup for the Soul*. Deerfield Beach, FL: Health Communications, 1993, pp.27-28.

Food for thought

What would others say about Christ and about your faith if they could see your attitude toward each other Christian in your life?

ACTS PRAYING

A - **ADORATION** - Take some time to praise God for who He is, identifying some of His attributes you find particularly meaningful. You may want to express your heart to Him in a journal.

C - **CONFESSION** - Remember, don't go looking for something to confess; that is introspection. Instead ask God to search your heart and to bring to mind anything that needs to be dealt with.

T - **THANKSGIVING** - Thank God for the many blessings of your life, taking a moment to ask God what you need to be thankful for.

S - **SUPPLICATION** - Pray for God to working in your life as you seek to assume your role in helping the body become the kind of community God desires. Bring to Him any requests and needs that are on your heart.

Day 3: A Debt of Love

"Owe nothing to anyone except to love one another; for he who loves his neighbor has fulfilled the law."

- Romans 13:8

How much debt do you carry? A little? A lot? None? The total American consumer debt (excluding mortgages and car loans) first topped $1 trillion in 1994. It has more than doubled since then. The average household has about $12,000 in this kind of debt.[7] The bottom line is that we owe a lot! Is this wrong? Some take Romans 13:8 to mean that a Christian should never have any debt under any circumstances. Actually, the word owe is in the present tense. The implication is that we should not keep owing someone a debt. In other words, if we have a debt we should pay it off. The balance should diminish. In truth, the point here isn't about finances at all – it is about love. Do you count love among your obligations? Paul is saying that this is the only kind of obligation whose balance doesn't diminish with each payment. Love is the permanent debt. There is a point of clarity we must not miss in Paul's words. When he speaks of love, he isn't just talking about how you feel toward others. Both uses of the word love in this verse are verbs – actions – not nouns. In other words, they are what we do, not what we possess.

Most think we have accomplished something worthy and laudable when we show love to others. We deserve a pat on the back, and if our deeds were especially benevolent, a trophy is in order. Not so, says Paul. When we show love, we haven't done the extraordinary. We are merely making payments on a debt we owe. The Pharisees taught to love your neighbor and hate your enemies. Jesus challenged

[7] http://www.creditcards.com/credit-card-industry-facts-and-personal-debt-statistics.php

this notion: "and if you love those who love you, what credit is that to you? For even sinners love those who love them" (Luke 6:32). God wants His people to be a community known by love – a commitment to love by choice, not feelings. Speaking of God, Jesus adds in Luke 6:35, "...for He Himself is kind to ungrateful and evil men." We only applaud ourselves for acts of love because we compare ourselves to each other. None of us consistently loves as God does.

A friend was in a tight spot. His marriage was on the rocks. As a last ditch hope, he agreed to counseling. The counselor asked, "Do you love your wife?" "What?" he exclaimed, "of course I love my wife!" The counselor began to read Paul's description of love from the Bible, "Love is patient, love is kind and is not jealous, love does not brag and is not arrogant, love does not act unbecomingly, it does not seek its own, is not provoked, does not take into account a wrong suffered, does not rejoice in unrighteousness, but rejoices with the truth; bears all things, believes all things, hopes all things, endures all things. Love never fails." "Do you love your wife?" he asked again. My friend hung his head and honestly admitted, "No." It was a hard pill to swallow, but truth helped him see that in both attitude and action he wasn't really loving her. That was a step in the right direction, but even more important was his realization that he didn't know God. You see, we cannot love others the way God wants without first experiencing His love for us. "...the fruit of the Spirit is love..." (Galatians 5:22). It is God who enables us to pay our debt of love.

Food for thought

Do you view love as doing something good or as a debt to be paid?

ACTS PRAYING

A - **ADORATION** - Take some time to praise God for who He is, identifying some of His attributes you find particularly meaningful. You may want to express your heart to Him in a journal.

C - **CONFESSION** - Remember, don't go looking for something to confess; that is introspection. Instead ask God to search your heart and to bring to mind anything that needs to be dealt with.

T - **THANKSGIVING** - Thank God for the many blessings of your life, taking a moment to ask God what you need to be thankful for.

S - **SUPPLICATION** - Pray for God to working in your life as you seek to assume your role in helping the body become the kind of community God desires. Bring to Him any requests and needs that are on your heart.

Day 4: The Source of Love

"Beloved, let us love one another, for love is from God; and everyone who loves is born of God and knows God."

- 1 John 4:7

We are supposed to love one another. We know that. But where does this love come from? Must we grit our teeth and try to make it happen? It is clear from John's words that being born of God is essential. Apart from being spiritually reborn, we are not capable of loving others with this kind of love. But John doesn't stop there. He also includes that one knows God as an enabling credential. While the two may appear as synonyms, the text clearly separates them. The word *born* in the original Greek is in the perfect tense. This means it is a completed act. The word *knows* is in the present tense and indicates an ongoing action. We must be a Christian to love as God loves, but we must also grow. We get to know God by spending time with Him, by obeying what He says, and by dealing with wrongs as He convicts us. The longer we pursue this relationship, the more we become like Him – the one who loves. John continues in verse 8, telling us, "The one who does not love does not know God, for God is love." If we are really going to love one another, we need to spend time with God who "is love." John tells us that "We love, because He first loved us" (1 John 4:19).

What does this kind of love look like? First John 4:9 tells us, "By this the love of God was manifested in us, that God has sent His only begotten Son into the world so that we might live through Him." God loved us by giving of Himself sacrificially to meet our needs. Again, this is more than just an example to follow; it is an enablement. Verse 10 continues, "In this is love, not that we loved God, but that He loved us and sent His Son to be the propitiation for our sins." God took the initiative. He "loved" us. He showed us grace. He didn't love us because we deserved it. He didn't love us because of anything we did. He simply chose to love us. All of this leads us to 1 John 4:11 – "Beloved, if God so loved us, we also ought to love one another." We are supposed to love one another, but not merely in the natural, human way. The natural way to love others is conditional love - "I love you because…" or "I love you if…". As Christians, if we only love conditionally, we are no different than the world. God wants us to love others because of Him, not because of them. He wants us to love unconditionally.

The subject of love was so important to John because he was gripped by the love of God. In his gospel, he repeatedly identifies himself as "the disciple whom Jesus loved" (Jn. 13:23; 19:26; 20:2; 21:7; 21:20). He uses the word love 109 times in his gospel and epistles. Love mattered to him because this former "son of thunder" had experienced being loved with God's love. We must draw on God's love to be able to love one another as we should. When we do, we help enable others to love. John closes out this thought in 1 John 4:12, saying, "No one has seen God at any time; if we love one another, God abides in us, and His love is perfected in us." Although no one has seen God, they can see Him in us if we love one another.

Food for thought

Are you drawing on God's love to be able to love others as you should?

ACTS PRAYING

A - **ADORATION** - Take some time to praise God for who He is, identifying some of His attributes you find particularly meaningful. You may want to express your heart to Him in a journal.

C - **CONFESSION** - Remember, don't go looking for something to confess; that is introspection. Instead ask God to search your heart and to bring to mind anything that needs to be dealt with.

T - **THANKSGIVING** - Thank God for the many blessings of your life, taking a moment to ask God what you need to be thankful for.

S - **SUPPLICATION** - Pray for God to working in your life as you seek to assume your role in helping the body become the kind of community God desires. Bring to Him any requests and needs that are on your heart.

Day 5: Fervently Love One Another

"Since you have in obedience to the truth purified your souls for a sincere love of the brethren, fervently love one another from the heart"

- 1 Peter 1:22

In his first epistle, Peter teaches that one of the consequences of having purified our souls by obedience to the truth is to the end that we have "a sincere love of the brethren" (1 Peter 1:22). The word sincere means a love that is not hypocritical or two-faced. Doesn't it break your heart when someone is two-faced? Paul exhorted in Romans 12:9, "let love be without hypocrisy." True love is always sincere, with no mixed motives. Peter states that our love should be fervent. The Greek word not only has the idea of intensity, but also of intentionality. Fervent love doesn't happen by accident and is not driven merely by feelings. The root idea is one stretching forward with all one's might like a runner at the finish line of a race. The clear message of Peter is that loving the brethren is not something we do whenever we get around to it; we must purpose to love. This idea of intentionality is echoed by the author of Hebrews: "…let us consider how to stimulate one another to love and good deeds." We should not only love each other, but we should devise ways to motivate each other toward love. Peter considers this message of fervency so important that he repeats it: "Above all, keep fervent in your love for one another, because love covers a multitude of sins" (1 Peter 4:8). When we are making the effort to love others, we make it easier for our own faults to be overlooked.

We have seen Christ repeatedly command us to love one another. We have seen Paul repeat this idea again and again in his epistles. (To the Corinthians: "Let all that you do be done in love" 1 Cor. 16:14; To the Colossians: "beyond all these things put on love, which is the perfect bond of unity" Col. 3:14). We have seen manifold exhortations to love from John, the disciple whom Jesus loved. Here we see Peter repeatedly calling us to fervently love one another. Why all this concern? The context of Peter's call in 4:8 to "keep fervent in your love for one another," is his reminder in 1 Peter 4:7, "The end of all things is near." Consider the following verses. Speaking of the end times, Jesus said, "Because lawlessness is increased, most people's love will grow cold" (Matthew 24:12). Paul warned that in the last days, "...men will be lovers of self, lovers of money...lovers of pleasure rather than lovers of God" (2 Timothy 3:2-4). The world has become a very selfish place. Unfortunately, Paul goes on to point out in the next verse that these are not people outside the church. These selfish people may not be Christians, but they are "holding to a form of godliness" (2 Timothy 3:5). The closer we get to Christ's return, the <u>more</u> we need to be fervent about loving one another.

Food for thought

Are you loving others intensely and intentionally?

ACTS PRAYING

A - **ADORATION** - Take some time to praise God for who He is, identifying some of His attributes you find particularly meaningful. You may want to express your heart to Him in a journal.

C - **CONFESSION** - Remember, don't go looking for something to confess; that is introspection. Instead ask God to search your heart and to bring to mind anything that needs to be dealt with.

T - **THANKSGIVING** - Thank God for the many blessings of your life, taking a moment to ask God what you need to be thankful for.

S - **SUPPLICATION** - Pray for God to working in your life as you seek to assume your role in helping the body become the kind of community God desires. Bring to Him any requests and needs that are on your heart.

ABOUT THE AUTHOR

Eddie Rasnake graduated with honors from East Tennessee State University. He and his wife, Michele, served seven years with Cru at the University of Virginia, James Madison, and as campus director at the University of Tennessee. Eddie left Cru to join Wayne Barber at Woodland Park Baptist Church where he still serves as Senior Associate Pastor. He has authored dozens of books and Bible studies and has published materials in Afrikaans, Albanian, German, Greek, Italian, Romanian, Russian and Telugu. Eddie and his wife Michele live in Chattanooga, Tennessee.

What Christian Leaders have to say about Eddie Rasnake's books:

"I encourage you to make these studies a part of your study of God's Word - I am confident you will be blessed!" – **Dr. Bill Bright**, Founder of Cru

"If you long to understand how God dynamically works in the lives of people like you and me, 'Following God' will be food for your soul." – **John MacArthur**, Pastor-Teacher, Grace Community Church

"These three dear men who love God and love His Word have produced an excellent study that will help you see in real life, flesh and blood examples, the cruciality of 'Following God' fully." – **Kay Arthur**, Executive Director, Precept Ministries International

"A wonderful resource for those who are serious in their Bible Study." – **Adrian Rogers**, Pastor, Bellevue Baptist Church, Memphis, Tennessee

"This study consistently takes the student to the Word of God. A refreshing study that stays true to scripture." – **Henry T. Blackaby**, co-author of Experiencing God

"Throughout my ministry of forty-one years, I have never read anything more fresh and enlightening than this book of knowing and living the will of God." – **Reverend Bill Stafford**, Evangelist, Director, International Congress on Revival

"I highly recommend this book not only to the new believer...but also to the older saint who would like a fresh look at how to discover God's will." – **Jan Silvious**, Author and Speaker

"You won't regret the time you spend reading Eddie Rasnake's book. I count it a privilege to know him personally and work with him. His book will help you read the signposts of decisions correctly and properly." – **Dr. Spiros Zodhiates**, Editor of The Hebrew/Greek Key Study Bible, President Emeritus, AMG International.

"If your heart's desire is to become a devoted follower of Christ, then 'Following God' will serve as a compelling roadmap." – **Joseph Stowell**, President Emeritus, Moody Bible Institute

"Fresh, original, imaginative – and Biblical – were the words that came to mind as I read 'What Should I Do, Lord?' Easy reading makes the principles accessible even to the newest Christian." – **Ron Dunn**, Author and Speaker

"Those who seek to do God's will often make decisions with lifelong impact. The tendency is to want to see our names written in the sky along with specific instructions as to what to do. Eddie Rasnake helps young and old alike understand how to know God's will by seeking God's way." – **Frank Brock**, President Emeritus, Covenant College